1756 – 1791?

*One for sorrow,
two for joy,
three for a girl,
four for a boy,
five for silver,
six for gold,
Seven for a secret never to be told.*

"The Magpie Rhyme"

And for centuries now, people have believed that a single magpie brings bad luck, but that magpies, in a pair, bring joy.

"A Secret Never to be Told" is based on real people, real events, and true stories, in the lives of two of the greatest composers the world has ever known.

Foreword

A conductor friend of an opera I was singing in, by the name of Eliano Mattiozzi, an Italian living in New Zealand, had suggested an idea to me one day after we had finished rehearsing the music of my role, Ferrando, in Opera New Zealand's production of Verdi's opera, 'Il Trovatore', two years before I had my heart by-pass operation.

"You're a writer, aren't you?" he asked me.

"Yes, "I said.

"What would you say if I told you Mozart didn't die on December 5, 1791? That he faked his death and lived on?" he said.

"I can think of a number of reasons why Mozart may have faked his death," I said, "… his debts, The Freemasons, his affairs, his wife… but if he'd lived on, he wouldn't have kept quiet. He would have composed music."

"He did and he didn't," he said. "He composed with and through someone else."

"Who?"

"Rossini."

"Gioacchino Rossini?"

"Yes. Gioacchino Antonio Rossini. I thought you might be interested in writing their story."

"… thought I might be interested?"

For the next two years, I researched the evidence for Eliano's claim, his assertion. One year focussing on Mozart, one year focussing on Rossini. But then, suddenly, tragically, during that time, Eliano died of a heart attack.

I finished the research just before my operation, and was looking around for someone I would be happy with to write the screenplay, using my research.

Without success.

And five weeks, five days and eighteen hours after my operation, I wrote the opening lines of the "Maestro" screenplay. And the words poured out of me. I couldn't stop them coming. It was like they were already there, sitting in my brain, and all I had to do was let them out. Six weeks later, I finished the first draft. It was a Friday. The next morning, Saturday morning, I started on my next story/screenplay. And that pattern, that condition, that obsession, that disease, has repeated itself, over and over, ever since. For over twenty years.

"A Secret Never to be Told" is the novel that came out of that "Maestro" screenplay: the story of Wolfgang Amadeus Mozart and Gioacchino Antonio Rossini, two of the greatest composers the world has ever known.

Lynn John

About the Author

Lynn John was born and educated in Wales and now lives in New Zealand. He is a writer of screenplays, stage-plays, television series for children and parents, novels, television drama series, short films, language and drama textbooks, travel articles, opera librettos, and a children's television animation series. He's an opera singer with New Zealand Opera. He trains male voice choirs. He was awarded a Winston Churchill Fellowship to record indigenous music in the Pacific.

Dedication

to my friend
Eliano Mattiozzi-Petralia
who gave me the idea

And my thanks and appreciation to John Grant
and to Virginia Cattell for their ideas and skills
in the design of the cover of this book

What if Mozart didn't die on December 5, 1791?

What if he lived on?

A Secret Never to be Told

A novel

by

Lynn John

Published by Filament Publishing Ltd
14, Croydon Road, Beddington,
Croydon, Surrey CR0 4PA
+44(0)20 8688 2598
www.filamentpublishing.com

"A Secret Never to be Told"
Lynn John

ISBN 978-1-915465-11-5
© 2022 Lynn John

The right of Lynn John to be identified as the author of this work has been asserted by him in accordance with the Designs and Copyrights Act 1988 Section 77

All rights reserved
No part of this work may be copied in any way without the prior written permission of the publisher

Table of Contents

Part One		**15**
One	Vienna, December 6, 1791	16
Two	Vienna, St Stephen's Cathedral	19
Three	Vienna, St Marx Cemetery	21
Four	Vienna, Grünangergasse apartments	23
Five	Vienna, December 10, 1791	31
Six	Italy, Pesaro, Papal States. February 29, 1792	33
Part Two		**35**
Seven	Italy, Pianoro. 1798	36
Eight	Italy, Baron van Swieten's house. 1798	38
Nine	Italy, Baron van Swieten's house	44
Ten	Italy, The public square. Pesaro	46
Part Three		**49**
Eleven	Italy, Il Teatro del Corso. Bologna. 1805	50
Twelve	Italy, Liceo Musicale. Bologna	53
Part Four		**55**
Thirteen	Northern Italy, A gypsy caravan	56
Fourteen	Italy, Il Teatro del Corso. Bologna	59
Fifteen	Italy, The Rossini home. Pesaro	61
Sixteen	Italy, Il Liceo Musicale. Bologna	64
Seventeen	Northern Italy, A public park	66
Part Five		**69**
Eighteen	Italy, Teatro Municipale. Ferrara	70

Part Six   79

Nineteen	Italy, Gioacchino's rooms. Ferrara	80
Twenty	Italy, La Scala. Milan	82
Twenty-one	Italy, Gioacchino's rooms. Ferrara	84
Twenty-two	Italy, La Scala. Milan	87
Twenty-three	Italy, Pianoro	90
Twenty-four	Italy, A room in Venice	93
Twenty-five	Italy, Gioacchino's and Maestro's room. Venice	96
Twenty-six	Italy, Venice to Naples	101
Twenty-seven	Italy, Teatro San Carlo. Naples	107
Twenty-eight	Italy, Isabella's drawing room. Naples	110
Twenty-nine	Italy, Teatro San Carlo. Naples	114
Thirty	Italy, Barbaja's apartment 210 Via Toledo, Naples	119
Thirty-one	Italy, The market in the teeming streets of Naples	123
Thirty-two	Italy, Backstage at Teatro San Carlo. Naples	125
Thirty-three	Italy, Barbaja's apartment in palazzo 210 Via Toledo. Naples	130
Thirty-four	Italy, Teatro San Carlo. Naples	133
Thirty-five	Italy, Teatro San Carlo. Naples	137
Thirty-six	Italy, Gioacchino's apartment in palazzo 210 Via Toledo. Naples	141
Thirty-seven	Italy, A caffè in Naples	156
Thirty-eight	Italy, Gioacchino's rooms 210 Via Toledo. Naples	162
Thirty-nine	Italy, Isobella's rooms. Naples	169
Forty	Italy, Rome	172
Forty-one	Italy, Rome	177
Forty-two	Italy, Pianoro	179

Forty-three	Italy, Rome	181
Forty-four	Italy, Gioacchino's rooms. Naples	186
Forty-five	Italy, Naples	192
Forty-six	Italy, Naples	195
Forty-seven	Italy, Maestro's home in Pianoro	199
Forty-eight	Italy, Isabella's villa in Castenaso	201
Forty-nine	Italy, Maestro's home in Pianoro	203
Fifty	Italy, A caffè in Naples	206

Part Seven — 210

Fifty-one	France, Le Théâtre-Italien. Paris	211
Fifty-two	France, A street in Paris	214
Fifty-three	France, Gioacchino and Isabella's apartment. Paris	217
Fifty-four	France, A theatre dressing-room at Paris Opera. Paris	220
Fifty-five	France, A restaurant. Rue de Rivoli. Paris	225
Fifty-six	France, Le Café Anglais. Paris	227
Fifty-seven	Northern Italy, A carriage on the open road	230
Fifty-eight	France, A street. Paris	232
Fifty-nine	France, A bordello. Paris	236
Sixty	France, Gioacchino and Isabella's apartment. Paris	237
Sixty-one	France, Maestro's apartment. Paris	238
Sixty-two	France, A public park. Paris	241
Sixty-three	France, Maestro's apartment. Paris	243
Sixty-four	France, Maestro's apartment. Paris	245
Sixty-five	In conclusion	249

A note from the author — 251

Part One

ONE

Vienna

December 6, 1791

A hooded figure, carrying a torch held low to light the way, hurries down a flight of stone steps. A puff of wind catches the flame and it flickers, threatening to go out. The figure stops, puts up a shading hand until the flame steadies, then continues down the gaping corridor. The figure enters a windowless room, closes the door, and throws off her hood and cape. The figure is five months pregnant.

She holds the torch high over a cheap, unadorned wooden coffin that sits on a trestle. She slots the torch into a wall bracket above the coffin and opens a bag she is carrying. She takes out a screwdriver and starts to unscrew the lid of the coffin.

There is a sharp clanging noise above and she freezes. Her eyes dart to the roof, as if she could see through it. She waits. And she waits. There is no further sound and she turns back to unscrewing the lid. Her hand is shaking and the screwdriver slips out of the groove in the screw and gouges the top of the coffin.

She licks her fingertips and brushes the gouge as if she could erase it, then attacks the screws again. She removes them, one by one.

The lid has three thumb-sized holes in the centre of its wider end, arranged in a triangle. She hooks her fingers into the holes, lifts and slides the lid off the coffin.

There is a man's body in the coffin. Brushed hair, powdered face, closed eyes, red cravat at the neck, and hands crossed over the chest. At peace. Suddenly the man opens his eyes wide and shoots his arms up at her. And grins.

"Magdalena!" he breathes.

Magdalena leans over him and kisses him full on the mouth. "It's time," she whispers, and she breathes warm, moist air over his blue lips.

With her help, the man sits up and climbs stiffly out of the coffin. She wraps him in a warm blanket and rubs hard. He shivers and starts to stutter speak but she signals him to silence. He obeys. He stamps his feet and blows on his hands. He wraps his arms around Magdalena and holds her.

They move to a bench in the corner of the room. The man reaches underneath the bench and pulls out a human arm. He tugs on it. A torso follows the arm. Together, they pull out the body of an unshaven, scruffily-clad male, about forty years old, and stand it up against the trestle. The body is stiff but it slides to the floor. They lift it again, then lever it up and into the vacated coffin. They force the arms to bend. so that they fit into the coffin.

Magdalena places the lid back on top of the coffin. They juggle it so that the lid holes match the holes in the sides of the coffin. It is too dark. They cannot see the holes. The man swears under his breath. Magdalena shakes her head and takes down the torch from its wall bracket and holds the flame over one of the holes in the lid. The man sticks the screwdriver into the hole and they juggle the lid until it slips into the hole below. He screws it into place, moves to the opposite side, jiggles and screws, till the lid is back in place.

TWO

Vienna

St Stephen's Cathedral

The coffin sits on its trestle in the curve of the entrance vestibule of St Stephen's Cathedral. The doors to the church proper are closed. The faint sounds of a male choir beyond, filter through the door.

There are nine mourners in the vestibule, including the priest. All male. Court Composer Salieri is standing at the back of the mourners, furthest away from the coffin. Salieri, Court Composer of the Emperor of Austria.

There is the sound of running footsteps on the flagstones, and a breathless Gottried van Swieten bursts into the vestibule. He stops dead when he sees the coffin, and gasps. "So, it's true!"

Gottfried turns to Salieri, "I didn't believe it! They told me and I didn't believe it! I saw him only yesterday! I talked to him only yesterday!"

Salieri is unmoved. He looks at van Swieten as if he were a stranger, an interloper off the street, even though they had both been members of the Holy Roman Emperor Joseph 11's Imperial court for many years together, had dined together, had intrigued together – often clashing it must be admitted – had even made music together. Because Salieri knows what had happened. On that same fateful yesterday. He knows what had happened in the new Imperial court, new since Joseph 11 had died, new since Joseph's brother, Leopold 11, had been crowned Holy Roman Emperor. Emperor Leopold had relieved Gottfried van Swieten of his commissions as Director of the State Education Commission and Director of The Censorship Commission, on that very same yesterday that Mozart had died.

Salieri turns away from van Swieten and says nothing. As if van Swieten wasn't there. Because, of course, van Swieten wasn't there any more. Very satisfactory.

The priest moves to the coffin, presses his fingertips together to form a pyramid, then crosses himself. He intones, "In nomine domini sui filique ite ad infernos".

He turns to face the mourners, and declaims, "Dear friends, we are gathered here today to mark the passing of a man who was like no other. A comet who burned in our skies so brightly, so fiercely, yet so briefly. Wolfgang Amadeus Mozart..."

THREE

Vienna

St Marx Cemetery

The coffin is sitting on a cart that is being pulled down the street by an aged, knackered horse. Four men accompany the cart, one in front holding the horse's bridle, two following closely, and a solitary man, further behind, Gottfried van Swieten. They have been walking the two and a half miles from St Stephen's Cathedral and are showing signs of exhaustion and the bitter cold. The cart approaches an open pit in the burial ground.

A carriage is stationed at the entrance to the grounds. As if waiting. The blinds of the carriage are drawn. Magdalena edges a corner of a blind to one side so that she can see. Wolfgang, at her side, and still wrapped in a blanket, presses forward, trying to see past her. She pushes him back from the light.

The cart stops parallel to the pit. The coffin is lifted out, levered to the pit edge, stood on its end, the lid moved to one side, and the body tipped over the edge into the pit, where it lies, face-down, with fifteen or so other corpses. A gravedigger shovels quicklime over the newly laid corpse.

Magdalena covers her face with a shawl, leans her head out the carriage door and calls, "Grünangergasse apartments, driver."

The carriage lurches off.

FOUR

Vienna

Grünangergasse apartments

Wolfgang and Magdalena enter the apartment, close the door, and turn to face one another. There is a moment of stillness and silence.

"It's illegal, isn't it?" says Magdalena.

"What is?" answers Wolfgang.

"To sleep with the dead."

"Oh, I don't know," he says. "You've been sleeping with that your husband of yours for years, haven't you?"

And he emits a wailing, baying laugh, then throws himself onto the bed, turning immediately onto his back, crossing his hands over his chest, and closing his eyes.

Magdalena shrieks and climbs on top of him.

He opens his eyes. It is still dark. A chink of breaking light is sneaking through a gap between the not-quite-closed curtains.

Magdalena is sleeping on her back and breathing with her mouth slightly open. Each time she breathes out, there is a little explosion of air.

Pop!

He waits for the next and counts. Like a pulse. Regular.

Pop!

"La vendetta …" he sings in a breathy whisper.

Pop! Fourth beat second bar.

"Oh, La vendetta …"

Pop! Fourth beat fourth bar.

A violoncello joins his singing, then a violin.

He stretches out his hand and cups her breast.

Pop!

He holds his hand still and watches for her reaction. There is no reaction. She sleeps and pops.

He gently massages the breast in slow circular motions.

Pop!

He touches the nipple.

And she misses the beat.

He knows she is holding her breath and watching him, even though he can't see her eyes. On the first beat of the next bar, he gently pulls the nipple out between his thumb and two fingers, like toffee. He releases it on the third beat. No reaction. He repeats, first beat next bar. The nipple starts to harden and swell.

"È bassezza, è ognor viltà …"

His hand slides to the other breast. The nipple is soft and supple.

He touches it twice, flicking it, only just, in half-beats. It becomes instantly erect.

And she begins to move her hips in an undulating movement.

"… Coll'astuzia, coll'arguzia …"

He flicks on the beat, rests a beat, then flicks again. And she swings her legs up and over, and sits astride him.

On the outskirts of Vienna, a heavily-clad rider, hat pulled down low over his face to keep out the wind and the cold, scarf wrapped tight around his neck, is galloping his horse pell-mell down a cobbled street. Urgent. Intent.

Magdalena moves on Wolfgang, up and slowly down, and gasps in rhythm with his moans.

The rider urges his stumbling mount down a narrow alleyway – almost knocking over an old man who cries out and scrambles out of the way.

Magdalena's eyes are closed tight, mouth wide open in a silent scream of joy.

The rider reins in his horse, dismounts in one movement, leaves the horse untethered, and dashes through a door.

Magdalena's joy falters as she becomes aware of pounding feet on stairs outside the room.

The door is flung violently open and the rider stands in the doorway, panting, sweating, wild-eyed.

Magdalena spins her head around, "Franz!" she screams.

"What?" cries Wolfgang from beneath her, not seeing, "What do you mean, 'Franz'?"

The rider lets out a howl and lunges towards them. He has a barber's razor in his hand. He slashes at Magdalena, opening up her face, neck and shoulders. Blood gushes onto the pinned Wolfgang. Magdalena falls to the bed beside him then rolls off onto the floor.

Franz drops to his knees beside her and continues to hack and slash. "Woman!" he roars. "Woman! No one will have you! You will die with me!" He sobs uncontrollably as he cuts and slashes at the screaming, writhing form of Magdalena.

Wolfgang throws himself at the slashing arm and they crash to the floor, locked together. With the impact they separate. Franz rolls away into the corner, heaving and sobbing, huddling over, facing the wall. Wolfgang staggers to his feet and stands over him, waiting for him to turn and rise. But Franz does not move. Wolfgang reaches out a hand nervously, tentatively, then suddenly grasps Franz by the shoulder and spins him around. Franz' throat is open from ear to ear.

"My God!" breathes Wolfgang.

He drops to his knees and holds his hands over the gaping wound trying to staunch the flow of blood. The blood pumps through his fingers, then slows, then stops. Wolfgang pulls his hands away. Franz is dead.

"Why Franz?" gasps Wolfgang. "Why, in God's name ...?"

Wolfgang staggers back from the body, and suddenly hears the sobbing Magdalena. He drops to her side. "Magdalena!" he whispers.

She does not answer.

He levers her up from the floor and sees the cuts and slashes and blood on her face, neck and shoulders. "Oh no!" He cradles her head in his arms. "Magdalena! Don't die... don't leave me. Not now – not after all we've done, not after..."

And he hears her voice, next to his face. "Shhh! Shhh!" she is saying, "Shhh! I won't leave you. I'm not going ..."

"Oh God, the baby!" cries Maestro. "What about the baby?"

"The baby ... will be fine ... it's too early ... stop, stop please, my love ..."

"He's dead, Magdalena. Franz is dead!

Magdalena stares at him. "How can he be dead?"

"I don't know how! But he is! He must have cut his own throat – I didn't do it – I swear, Magdalena. I didn't – you must believe me!"

"It makes no difference ... whether you did or you didn't... either way he's not ..."

"Hollo! Is everything alright in there?" A man's voice from outside the door. "I heard screaming and shouting!"

"A doctor!" cries Magdalena. "Someone's hurt ... quick ... get a doctor!"

"Can I help? Do you want me to come in and ...?"

"No!" screams Magdalena. "A doctor! Get a doctor! Run, you fool!"

There are sounds of footsteps rapidly retreating down the stairs.

"Quick ... lock the door!"

"I swear, Magdalena, I didn't hurt him ..."

"The door! Lock the damned door!"

Wolfgang scrambles to his feet and fumbles with the key which quickly becomes covered in blood. It slips to the floor. He scrambles and picks it up and finally gets it into the lock. He turns it.

"Now the razor ..." she gasps, "... find the razor and put it in his hand."

"The razor?"

"Aah!" she screams in pain and frustration, "Do it! Do it now, before the fool comes back!"

The razor is nowhere to be seen. Wolfgang levers Franz' body from the floor. A fresh gout of blood spurts from the neck as he moves it. There. Under his head. Wolfgang retrieves it and searches for Franz' hand. Right hand. He pulls it from under his twisted body. He lays the razor carefully in the hand as if he does not want to hurt it. The razor falls out.

"It won't stay! It just falls out!"

"Make it!" gasps Magdalena.

Wolfgang turns Franz' hand over so that it is facing upwards, pays the razor on it and forces the fingers closed over it. "Yes!" he exclaims out loud. Too loud.

"Shhh ... now go ..." says Magdalena.

"Go?"

"Yes, go! Out the window ... it's ... it's a drop ... but you'll be safe."

"I can't! I can't run away while you're bleeding like this! You are badly hurt …"

Magdalena heaves herself up onto her hands, "You can and you must!" She sags and falls back against the wall. "No one … is going to believe … you didn't kill him if they find you here …"

"But I didn't …"

"They won't believe it!" she screams and cries out with the pain of it, "… how can you … be here anyway? You're dead, remember?"

"Magdalena!"

"You're lying at the bottom of a pit … covered in lime, remember?"

"I can't leave you like this!"

"If you don't … then it will all have been for nothing … nothing!"

There are footsteps and voices outside the door.

"Go now! Go!" she gasps.

With a strangled cry, Wolfgang turns to the window and forces it open. He puts a leg through then brings it back in again. "Magdalena, I can't do it."

The door handle is rattled violently and a man's voice, the same man's voice as before, shouts, "It's locked! The door is locked. I've got a doctor!"

Another man's voice yells, "Break it down, you fool! Here, let me!" and there are sounds of bodies crashing against the door.

"Please Maestro, please," begs Magdalena, "… for me … for us!"

Maestro scrambles out the window and drops from view. There is another crash of bodies against the door and it bursts open. Four men rush into the room.

Magdalena's eyes are closed.

A doctor is cradling her head against his shoulder. "Can you hear me?" he asks.

There is no response from Magdalena.

"Pass me the smelling salts," he orders.

A man hands him a bottle from a bag lying on the floor. The doctor applies salts to Magdalena's nose. Her head jerks back and she opens her eyes.

"What happened here?" he asks.

Magdalena stares at him and says nothing.

"Can you speak?" he says.

Magdalena slowly shakes her head from side to side.

"Did he kill himself? The man here – with his throat … he cut you, right? Then what?"

Magdalena stares at him then begins to cry. She coughs and shudders, clearly in great pain.

"The bellows, man! Pass me the bellows, there, quick!" cries the doctor.

The man passes him a pair of bellows from the hearth.

The doctor carefully inserts the nozzle into Magdalena's mouth and begins to squeeze, gently, pumping air into her lungs. Magdalena's eyes widen with each pump, but she stares straight ahead, in silence, uttering not a single word.

FIVE

Vienna

December 10, 1791

Viennese newspapers publish the news of Franz Hofdemel's attack on his wife, and his suicide, as occurring on December 10, 1791, four days after the actual event.

Those who knew the real date and day of the attack and suicide wonder why. Some speculate that it was deliberate in order to distance the attack and mutilation of Wolfgang Amadeus' pupil, Magdalena Hofdemel, and the suicide of her husband, Franz, from Mozart's own death, because reports suggest that Franz had been heard to call out before he killed himself, that if he couldn't have her, then no one would.

Others wonder if the Empress Maria Luisa, wife of the Holy Roman Emperor, Leopold 11, who befriended the injured Magdalena after the attack, who helped her recover, had perhaps intervened and influenced the newspaper reports.

Rumours and gossip are rife.

Franz Hofdemel's body is ordered to be sewn into a cow's skin and thrown into an unmarked pit by a public hangman, the designated burial for all sinners who kill themselves.

But the corpse is examined by surgeon, Johann Christian Sartori, who does not agree with such a barbaric and shameful act, especially given the dire medical state of the surviving wife. He directs that it is to be buried, with dignity, in an unmarked, unknown grave.

SIX

Italy

Pesaro, Papal States. February 29, 1792

Giuseppe Rossini kneels in prayer in front of the twelve statuettes of the Apostles which are lined up in a row on the window-sill of the living room that is kitchen, dining room, music room, of his two-roomed house. He is very agitated, praying and crossing himself repeatedly.

"Help her, Blessed Mother!" he pleads. "I beg you. Help my Anna through this time. She has been in labour for two days now, Blessed Mother. She is in great pain, Blessed Mother. I am in great pain, Blessed Mother. Help us, I beseech you. And let it be a boy, Blessed Mother ... I have named him already, Blessed Mother. He is to be Gioacchino – Gioacchino Antonio Rossini!" He stops, listens and then nods. "I know what you are saying, Blessed Mother – yes, he could be a girl. This is possible. I know this. But I will make you a deal, Blessed Mother.

I will dedicate my life to you.

I will light a candle to you every day ... two candles ... no, six candles every day, Blessed Mother, if you will just help my Anna now, in her moment of …"

There is a loud cry of pain from the adjoining room. Giuseppe leaps to his feet and snatches up his walking stick and, with a louder cry of his own, brings the stick smashing down on one of the Apostle statuettes. It shatters into pieces.

Anna cries out again and again from the adjoining room and each time she cries, in a frenzy, Giuseppe smashes another statuette, and another, and another, until they are all broken, and then, a miracle – when the last is smashed, Anna's cries stop, only to be replaced almost immediately by the cry of a new-born baby.

Giuseppe crosses himself feverishly, "Thank you, Blessed Mother, thank you, thank you, thank you." He looks up at the ceiling and throws his arms wide in welcome, "Gioacchino!"

Part Two

SEVEN

Italy

Pianoro. 1798

Wolfgang is cooking and dancing. A pasta and a minuet. One of his own, of course, K.604. A 'turning dance' for two, except that Wolfgang's partner is his pasta bowl. He and his bowl whirl in fast three-four time, like a rough and tumble peasant romp. He stirs the sauce while whirling, and spills a good serving onto the floor. His audience, Magdalena, little Therese, and young Franz, burst out laughing. They are echoed immediately by a baying Wolfgang.

Wolfgang moves behind Magdalena, bends and kisses the white scars on her neck and face – then fondles her hair from behind – running his fingers through the tresses – twisting and turning the hair – touching with the finger tips of one hand – and a piccolo dances in time with his fingers – then a flute joins in as he brings the fingers of his other hand in to play – and it becomes a dancing duet. Magdalena turns her head, sufficient to look up at him, and knows instinctively what he is doing and dreaming, and smiles.

Wolfgang slows his fingers, and the music dies away, and

eventually stops.

He moves back into the kitchen. He sweeps the spilled pasta into a basin, adds the rest of the unspoiled pasta, opens the door to the garden, and tosses the lot out onto the grass, for the chickens. The chickens cluck and fuss and gobble.

And Wolfgang decides to make a dessert instead. He breaks four eggs into a bowl and beats them furiously, but in time of course.

EIGHT

Italy

Baron van Swieten's house. 1798

It is Baron Gottfried van Swieten's birthday. Six guests, including Wolfgang and Magdalena, are seated around the large formal drawing room, drinking and talking. The Baron is standing near the fireplace.

Magdalena approaches him, gives him a beautifully-wrapped book and kisses him on the cheek. "I wish you many, many more birthdays to come, dear friend."

"Not too many, I hope my dear Magdalena, otherwise it could become very boring," he replies.

Wolfgang moves to the harpsichord and sits. "Gottfried!" he calls. They all turn to face him.

Magdalena starts in alarm and tries to signal "No" to him with a shake of the head, but Wolfgang seems or chooses not to see her.

"I cannot let your birthday go by, dear Gottfried," he says, "without someone playing something from what I know is one of your favourites – Bach's 'Well Tempered Clavier', yes?"

The Baron glances at Magdalena and smiles at her in reassurance, crosses to Wolfgang at the harpsichord, and rests his hand on Wolfgang's shoulder, "Yes, my friend, it is indeed a favourite."

"I've heard it said," says Wolfgang, "that when the angels go about their task of praising God, they play only Bach," and he plays the opening of Bach's 'Well Tempered Clavier' beautifully, delicately, sensitively, to everyone's delight, then pauses, both hands suspended in the air above the keyboard, and says, "But when the angels get together for fun of an evening… they play Mozart!" and his hands crash down onto the keyboard as he plays a manic, Mozartian version of what he has just played – with harsh chromaticisms and complex inversions and strettos, and then, when he finishes, he emits his wailing, baying laugh.

There are looks of amazement on the faces of the other four guests – but the suddenly frightened van Swieten moves quickly to usher them out of the drawing-room, while Magdalena slams the lid of the piano closed.

Magdalena and Wolfgang are sitting opposite one another in the kitchen of Wolfgang's house. Van Swieten is seated at the far side of the room, separate from them, but listening, impassive, head bowed.

There is a long silence which Wolfgang finds very difficult. He fidgets. He looks at Magdalena, then at van Swieten, then at his hands. And fidgets.

"Is it so easy to forget?" asks Magdalena, very quietly.

Wolfgang continues to fidget with his hands but he says nothing.

"Is it?" demands Magdalena.

Wolfgang looks down but still says nothing.

"You died – remember that?" Magdalena stands and stares at him. "And your wife didn't even attend your funeral! Nor the burial! She even refused to erect a headstone to mark your grave!"

Wolfgang flicks his eyes at van Swieten. Van Swieten remains impassive.

"Not only that," cries Magdalena, "she was sleeping with your pupil Sussmayr! She had his child!"

"You were carrying my child too Magdalena – and we were sleeping together…"

This too much for Magdalena. "Don't you think I know that?" She makes a huge effort to control herself and her temper. When she is breathing normally again, she carries on. "You owed money to everyone – your tailor, your wig-maker, your landlord – even your laundress… "all hammering on your door for their money!"

Wolfgang turns to look at van Swieten. "I've never been good with money…it seems to slip from …"

"You angered the Freemasons! You exposed their rituals in your silly little Magic Flute…"

"Silly little Magic …" he suddenly remembers who van Swieten is… "I meant no harm, Gottfried! I swear I didn't – I thought the Masons would like people to know …"

"… you bought a pauper's body!" Magdalena is relentless. "You tipped it into your coffin!"

Wolfgang stands too and hurls back at her, "They were poisoning me! Your dear husband Franz was supplying the aqua toffana and my darling wife, Stanzi, was pouring the stuff down my throat!"

"You do remember!" she says, suddenly quiet, suddenly a friend, "Well, well! And what about us? And our baby? Do you remember us too?"

"Of course I remember you!"

"Do you?" she said, still ominously quiet. "Do you really? Then what were you thinking when you were playing your little 'Oh isn't Maestro a clever little boy' game on the harpsichord last night?" and she is shouting again, "That the other guests were deaf and blind? That they wouldn't put two and two together and make Mozart? Is that what you wanted? You wanted people to know the truth? You want us discovered? Arrested for goodness' knows what – for murder?" She leans across the table at him. And he sits. "Is that it? Is that what you want?"

"You know it isn't what I want! But… but if I can't play, if I can't live my music, if I can't write …" He stands. "if I can't even fart in tune… I'll, I'll blow up!" He giggles and looks across at van Swieten.

Van Swieten remains impassive.

Magdalena sits and closes her eyes. Then she opens them, stands and walks across to van Swieten and stands against the wall. Van Swieten gets to his feet, moves to the kitchen table, pulls up her chair and sits facing Wolfgang.

Wolfgang looks at him nervously.

Van Swieten smiles. "My friend, you are the greatest composer who has ever lived. Your gifts come direct from God."

"I know," says Wolfgang, softly, earnestly.

"But sometimes you are a fool."

"I know," says Wolfgang, softly, earnestly.

"You risk yourself, and everyone you love, every time you say something, play something, write something that the world will hear and see, and cry, "Wolfgang Amadeus Mozart!"

"But I must, Gottfried. I cannot live without music. Every day I do not play, do not write, is like a death. Worse – because the music goes on – here! – in my head! It never stops! From the moment I wake till the moment I sleep. It's like God is punishing me! Here's your sentence, Wolfgang – create but keep it hidden, compose with my voice – but bury it within that pauper's corpse! I cannot, Gottfried. I cannot go on!" And he cries quietly, to himself.

Magdalena starts to go to him but stops herself and returns to the wall.

"But you can," says van Swieten.

"What?"

"You can compose, you can create, you can hear it sung and performed …"

"But you said …"

"… through someone else. Through a cypher, a surrogate, a protégé… call him what you will. You can write the loveliest of music and publish it in another's name. Does it matter whose name is on it? We will know. You will know." He leans in closer to Wolfgang, conspiratorial. "We can find some talented boy, a young man … for you to tutor, help, guide, publish through, live through – and the music of Wolfgang Amadeus Mozart will live on, and on, and on …"

And Wolfgang mouths softly, "Wolfgang Amadeus …"

"You can stay in this house rent free, and when I die, I'll leave it, and an annuity, to you both."

"Let's not talk of dying, dear Gottfried," breaks in Magdalena.

"No one lives for ever, my dear, not even Wolfgang Amadeus Mozart."

Magdalena moves to the table and lays her hands on Wolfgang's shoulders. "Think of it, my love – Salieri and all the other Italians at the court have been rejoicing and crying, 'He's gone! He's out of our lives!' – you will have the ultimate answer, the ultimate joy of showing them just how petty and silly their own little scribblings are – by composing from the dead! Just think of it …"

NINE

Italy

Baron van Swieten's house

A twelve-year-old boy is escorted into Gottfried van Swieten's drawing-room by his father. The boy is very nervous. So is the father. The boy is encouraged to sit at the harpsichord. He is reluctant. The father sits on the edge of a chair, and urges the boy forward. The boy sits at the harpsichord.

Wolfgang moves to stand just outside the drawing room door, in the hallway, where he can hear but not see, or be seen.

The boy begins to play an extract from a Mozart minuet. He plays slowly, with infinite care, frightened of making a mistake. It is a dirge.

Wolfgang throws his hands in the air, cries out "Salieri!" and disappears out the front door.

A confident, well-dressed young protégé is playing the violin in the same drawing room. He is confident – over-confident – and becomes increasingly flamboyant in his playing. He makes a slight error, stops, giggles like a young girl, and flutters his eyelashes at van Swieten.

Wolfgang wiggles out the door, waving goodbye as he goes.

A large, fat, young man, with an unfortunate rash of pimples on his face and neck, enters the room. He is carrying a large-bore basset horn. He sits, takes an alto-clarinet mouthpiece from a pocket, blows down the mouthpiece, sending a fine spray of spittle into the air, attaches the mouthpiece to the horn, and blows down the horn, producing a loud, fart sound… and we hear a maniacal, wailing, baying laugh from a retreating Wolfgang Amadeus Mozart.

TEN

Italy

The public square. Pesaro

Six-year-old Gioacchino Rossini is sitting in the back row of the Pesaro town band. The band's conductor is his father, Giuseppe Rossini. Giuseppe plays a trumpet in one hand and conducts with the other.

Gioacchino is holding a lista, a triangular strip of bent steel, high in the air. He is counting to himself, waiting, waiting for the exact moment to strike the instrument with a metal bar which he holds high in his other hand. The moment arrives and Gioacchino strikes once, hard, loud and clear.

Giuseppe throws both hands out and stops the band mid-note. He turns and indicates Gioacchino with a flourish of his hands and trumpet. "Gentlemen!" he cries, "I present to you my son, Gioacchino Antonio Rossini!"

All the members of the band turn, to face Gioacchino. They lay their instruments down, and, as if still being conducted, applaud Gioacchino.

A figure sits, head down, wrapped in a cloak, at the base of a pillar which is in the centre of a colonnade of pillars that lines one side of Pesaro piazza. It is cold. It is dark. The ground is unforgivingly hard, yet the figure sleeps.

A dog barks.

The figure stirs, spits into the gutter, unstops then swigs from a brandy flask at his side, and stands. He loosens his breeches and urinates into the gutter. He looks up at the sky as he sprays up and down the gutter with practised ease, and sees the first light of dawn breaking.

He ties up his breeches and makes his way across the square to the house of the Rossinis. He lets himself in the unlocked door, crosses to a bed in the corner of the living room and approaches the sleeping boy. He rouses him roughly. "Come!" he says, and turns and walks out of the house.

Gioacchino hurries behind him, pulling up his breeches and pushing in his shirt as he runs.

They enter a schoolroom. The room contains a spinet and a chair. Without a word being said, Gioacchino sits at the spinet, hands at his sides, and waits.

Prinetti sits on the floor with his back against the far wall and wraps himself in his cloak again. He closes his eyes. "Play," he mutters, as if reluctant to speak, as if annoyed that he has to speak at all.

And Gioacchino plays. He plays scales, endlessly progressing up the spinet and down again. After ten minutes of scales, Gioacchino tests Prinetti by pausing midway on a scale, watching and listening for Prinetti to react, then completing the scale and starting the next, then pausing again. When he is sure Prinetti is asleep, Gioacchino creeps out the door.

Gioacchino crosses the square and enters his house, gets back into bed, and closes his eyes.

In the blaze of a forge, the blacksmith hammers on a shoe, turns it, hammers, dips it into a hissing barrel of water, and hammers again.

A sweating, red-faced Gioacchino pumps on the bellows that heat the coals, making the fire flare and spark.

"More heat, Gioacchino!" bawls the smithy.

Gioacchino redoubles his efforts. The sparks fly and scatter.

Giuseppe Rossini and tutor Prinetti stand in the doorway, side by righteous side, arms folded, nodding, glowering at Gioacchino. Gioacchino does not look at them. He watches the flying sparks.

Gioacchino stands, hidden behind a pillar in the vestry of the Church in Pesaro. He stares fixedly at the cruets that hold the bread and the wine for the coming Mass. He waits and watches until he is certain no one is near, then creeps forward on tip-toe. He tips a cruet of wafers into his hands and crams them all into his mouth and chews furiously. Then, with his mouth still full of wafer, he lifts a cruet of wine to his lips and swigs. He chews and swigs until the cruets are all empty.

Then he is sick on the flagstone floor.

Part Three

ELEVEN

Italy

Il Teatro del Corso. Bologna. 1805

The theatre is full. Fourteen-year-old Gioacchino is seated in the orchestra pit next to his keyboard teacher, Zanotti.

Twenty-one-year-old Spanish dramatic soprano, Isabella Colbran, walks onto the stage. The audience greets her rapturously.

Gioacchino leaps to his feet the instant he sees her. Isabella curtsies low, almost spilling her heavy, exposed breasts into Gioacchino's hands. Gioacchino stares open-mouthed, forgetting to breathe. She is more than beautiful, in his hot, sweaty, fourteen-year-old, masturbating life, Isabella is every woman he has ever dreamed of. La Stupenda!

She is wearing a silk, red, figure-hugging gown, which flares, Flamenco-style, from the knees down. She is so tall, towering there just above him on the stage. She has blazing, obsidian-black eyes, a forest of raven-black hair, pinned at the front with a diadem, and an oval, perfectly balanced face. His eyes move down her body, inch by impossibly voluptuous inch. And he catches her nipples trying hard, so very hard, to burst through the restraining bodice. He wills them on. He moves down to her sucked-in waist, onto her swelling hips and mounds and crevices and, he knows, hidden, raven-black hair, the like of which he can only imagine.

Zanotti hisses at Gioacchino to sit. He is the only person, apart from Isabella, who is standing. Gioacchino seems not to hear.

"Sit down, Gioacchino!" he hisses more loudly.

"Who is she?" breathes Gioacchino.

"Isabella Colbran. She's Spanish. Now, sit down!"

Gioacchino ignores him and continues to stand. Isabella waits for the audience to become quiet, deathly quiet and still. Then, when she is satisfied, she turns her head towards Zanotti at the piano. Her eyes widen slightly in surprise at the sight of the standing boy, but then she smiles and nods for Zanotti to begin.

Zanotti tugs hard on the bottom of Gioacchino's jacket and forces him to sit. Zanotti plays the introduction to Carolina's aria from Cimarosa's "Il matrimonio segreto", and out of the mouth of Isabella come the most glorious, the most seductive sounds that Gioacchino or anyone else in the audience, he is sure, has ever heard – the richness, the smoothness, the power, the technical brilliance – and over an extraordinary three-octave range. It is too much for Gioacchino. He misses the page turn. Zanotti hisses and flips the page over himself. And all the other page turns.

As soon as the aria ends, Gioacchino abandons Zanotti and rushes out the side door and into the stage wings, where he waits.

Isabella comes off-stage to tumultuous applause. She stands side-stage, close to Gioacchino, at least a head taller than him, and oblivious of him. She poises, ready to go back on before the clapping starts to fade. She pulls a handkerchief from between her breasts and wipes the perspiration on her neck and in the valley between her breasts. Gioacchino stares at her glistening skin, so close that he could touch if he dared. Isabella turns to face the stage, ready. She hands the handkerchief to Gioacchino, without looking at him, barks, "Hold this," and disappears back onto the stage.

Gioacchino lifts the moist handkerchief to his nose and inhales deeply, then slowly, sensuously, he wipes his face and neck with it.

"Isabella!" he breathes. He tucks the handkerchief carefully down the front of his breeches. "I am in love!" he declares to himself, and wraps the handkerchief around his genitals.

Isabella rushes off-stage, flushed and happy. She thrusts her hand out towards Gioacchino, without looking at him, and snaps, "Thank you!"

"It's gone," says Gioacchino.

Isabella turns to look at him for the first time.

"What do you mean, 'It's gone'?"

"I ... I must have dropped it – and now I can't find it."

Isabella stares at him for one withering second, then brushes past him, muttering, "Stupid boy!" and heads for her dressing room.

Gioacchino watches her go, then slides his hand down the front of his breeches onto the handkerchief, and holds it there.

TWELVE

Italy

Liceo Musicale. Bologna

Gioacchino is sitting at the piano, hands at his sides, head down, as his teacher, Gian Zanotti, walks and talks, tapping the piano every now and then with a baton-like stick, and swishing dangerously close to Gioacchino's back and head.

"My dear Gioacchino, please excuse me for interrupting your gifted thoughts …" he brings the stick crashing down onto the stool next to Gioacchino's quivering thigh, "… but it's not good enough! You cannot rely on your natural ability to play – which you can claim no credit for, which you didn't earn, which God, for some totally misguided reason, blessed you with. You must study! You must understand the theory and only then will know what the composer wants. It is not enough just to play! Do you understand me? You are running when you should be walking. You must sweat! You must struggle! Just like the rest of us!"

Gioacchino nods to Zanotti and places his tongue between the swellings of Isabella's breasts just in time to catch the lucky bead of sweat that is trickling its outrageous way down the valley, intent on reaching the forested belly below.

Part Four

THIRTEEN

Northern Italy

A gypsy caravan

The gypsy woman's skin is like leather that has been weathered on the back of a horse. The furrows are deep and dark. The ridges shine. She lifts her head to look Wolfgang in the eye.

He stares back at her, unwavering.

She takes a tasselled cloth off a crystal ball.

Wolfgang shakes his head and stretches out both hands, palm up on the table.

The gypsy takes his right hand in both of hers and peers closely at it, then indicates his other hand. She studies it with equal intensity.

"Everything you touch, everything you do," she says, without taking her eyes off the hands, "is a wonder, a marvel – beyond the dreams of men. Your name is passed from mouth to mouth and will be, for many generations to come."

Magdalena draws in her breath sharply and leans in closer to the hands so that she can see for herself.

Wolfgang has not moved. "But the future?" he says. "What is to come?"

"The same as what has already been."

"What do you mean 'the same'?"

"I can only tell you what I see, my friend." She turns the hands over and studies the backs just as intently. "I see success," she says, "undreamt-of success, but ..." and she stops.

"But what?"

She releases the hands. "I see no happiness. I see no joy. I see only creation and pain." She looks up at him. "You have never been happy. You never will be happy. Because ... there is no line, here or here!" and she stabs her finger into his palms.

"What do you mean 'No line'?"

"No sun line – no groove – no line of joy. Look!" She grasps his forefinger and traces it down a deep line in the palm of her own hand. Then she switches her grip, turns his hand over, and shows him his palm. "No sun line – nothing!"

Wolfgang snatches his hands away and stares at the palms. He grasps her hands and pulls them close to his face, almost as if he were smelling them.

She smiles.

Wolfgang drops her hands and reaches inside his topcoat. He brings out a knife.

The gypsy starts back, wide-eyed, in fear.

Magdalena gasps.

Wolfgang lays his left hand, palm-up on the table, and carefully cuts a groove into the palm. Blood spurts and runs.

Magdalena cries out.

The gypsy stands and backs away.

Then with his blood-gushing left fist wrapped tightly around the knife handle, Wolfgang cuts a groove in his right hand. He drops the knife and spreads both hands open so they can see.

"Look!" he says, "sun lines."

FOURTEEN

Italy

Il Teatro del Corso. Bologna

Fourteen-year-old Gioacchino is standing side-stage. He is dressed in blouse and breeches, waiting to go on. He is playing Adolfo, young son of Camilla and Duca Alberto in Ferdinando Paer's opera "Camilla".

"Stand by Gioacchino!" whispers the stage manager.

Gioacchino nods without looking. He is watching the action onstage intently.

Two sopranos are singing. Both are in their thirties. One, Chiara Leon, is plain and flat-chested, the other, Anna Cittadini, is full-figured, with bulging, overflowing breasts.

Gioacchino stares. He can see nothing but the breasts.

Plain Chiara Leon turns to face the offstage Gioacchino, sings "Adolfo!", and opens her arms to greet him.

Gioacchino enters at a run, skirts around the waiting arms of flat-chested Chiara, and throws himself onto Anna's heaving bosoms. He buries his face in the breasts, nuzzling and kissing and licking them with obvious relish. Anna jumps back in surprise but Gioacchino hangs on and a nipple pops out of Anna's bodice. Gioacchino cannot believe his luck and zeros in on it, sucking it in till it's all gone.

The conductor stops, arms poised in the air, as he waits for Gioacchino, as Adolfo, to sing his line. Flat-chested Chiara hauls on Adolfo's head in a rough, seeming embrace, pulling him off Anna's breast. The nipple pops out of his mouth, and a flushed, puffed, but absolutely delighted-with-himself Gioacchino, sings, "Papa, where are you leading me?"

Anna Cittadini hoists her bodice high and the lucky, bright red nipple disappears from sight. She exits side-stage hurriedly, hissing to the stage manager as she passes him, "Make sure you have a bucket of cold water ready tomorrow night for that fourteen-year-old goat!"

FIFTEEN

Italy

The Rossini home. Pesaro

Giuseppe Rossini, Gioacchino Rossini, and uncle Francesco, are seated at the dinner table, each sipping a dark red chianti, even young Gioacchino, and all three nodding in appreciation. Anna Rossini is in the kitchen, tossing pasta and sauce in a large bowl. Satisfied, she carries her famed pasta amatriciana to the table. She places it in front of Uncle Francesco.

Francesco ladles a good portion into his own dish then passes the bowl onto Gioacchino. Gioacchino ladles out a larger portion into his dish, goes to pass the bowl on to the now seated Anna, changes his mind, and adds a little more to his already overflowing dish, then passes the bowl on to Anna. He starts eating immediately, not waiting for the others, cramming his mouth full. His mother looks at him disapprovingly but says nothing.

She takes a modest portion and passes on to Giuseppe.

Giuseppe places the serving bowl squarely in front of himself, and starts to eat straight from the bowl.

"I mean," says Francesco, mouth full, "Gioacchino here is fourteen years old. If you were to do it now, before … you know … before they drop, then he could be living in luxury, like a king, for the rest of his life."

"What do you mean, Uncle Francesco?" asks Gioacchino, "before what drop?"

"He means your voice, Gioacchino," says Anna, "before your voice breaks."

"He means your balls, Gioacchino," says Giuseppe.

"But it's going to have to be soon," says Francesco, "judging by the way he was burying his nose in those wonderful tits last night. God, they were like over-ripe melons, weren't they?"

Anna sniffs.

"The boy has a beautiful voice, Anna. Why lose it? Why not preserve it forever and become rich in the process? The boy is sitting on a fortune!"

Giuseppe bursts out laughing. Francesco stares at him then realizes he has made a joke and roars and pats Giuseppe, as if he intended it all along.

"And what, Francesco," says Anna, ignoring the laughter, "would a brother of mine, who is a butcher by trade, know about such things?

"I know about balls, Anna. And I know about Velluti, the castrato."

"The castrato?" says Gioacchino.

Francesco leans in close to him. There is a generous length of spaghetti hanging from his moustache. It is covered in Anna's famous tomato sauce and has a knob of prosciutto stuck to the end. "Yes, Giambattista Velluti. No balls – but what a voice!" He sucks the strand in. "He lives in a palace, is driven around in his own four-horse carriage, is asked to sing at the courts of princes and bishops. God's blood! He's even performed for Emperor Napoleon Buonaparte himself, and, listen to this, Gioacchino, he's loved and wanted and pursued by every woman who hears him and meets him."

Gioacchino stops eating. "… loved and wanted by every woman…" he repeats in awe. "Would it hurt, uncle Francesco?"

"Hurt? God's blood, no! Snip, snip, wouldn't feel a thing – you'd be over it in days."

"In days?" breathes Gioacchino.

"Days," says Francesco.

"No," says Anna.

"Think of it, Giuseppe – the brilliance, the purity, the clarity of this boy's voice but in a man's body – think of the power…"

Anna stands, the serving spoon in her hand, "No! I said. Are you listening? Never! Not for any money! Not while I live!" And she glares at Francesco for suggesting it, and at Giuseppe for not stopping it, and at Gioacchino for lusting at it. "Do I make myself clear?"

Silence, then, one by one, the three males resume eating their pasta.

SIXTEEN

Italy

Il Liceo Musicale. Bologna

Gioacchino and Dorinda Caranti, a female student of the same age, are singing a duet.

Gioacchino reaches and holds a top 'E'. It rings like a bell, albeit small bell, a bell that you could hold in one hand. Bellissimo. He repeats the note, expands on it, and the note suddenly cracks into baritone.

Pianist and singers stop.

There is a strangled, baying laugh from a man sitting at the back of the hall. The man cuts the laugh short and drops his head, bends and searches for his hat on the floor.

Silence.

Except for the muffled sound of a woman in the front row who is weeping. Anna Rossini.

Giuseppe Rossini and Uncle Francesco sit either side of her, faces of stone. Francesco's right cheek quivers and he turns to face Giuseppe on his left, and then Anna on his right. Neither of them looks at him. And not a word is said.

The audience applauds, uncertainly, like rain spitting at a window. Gioacchino resumes his singing, without another single cracked note. But it is not the same.

SEVENTEEN

Northern Italy

A public park

The ground is covered in russet leaves. Wolfgang scuffs and sweeps them aside with his feet as he walks, head-down, through the trees. His bandaged hands are tucked under his armpits to keep out the cold. He stops under a tree and leans against the trunk. He looks up at a single, solitary, red-turning-brown leaf that is still attached to a branch of the tree. He nods to it.

There is a group of people in the near distance – two women and a man. He can see them talking but cannot hear them. Their mouths open and close, all three at the same time. And he hears Fiordiligi, Dorabella and Don Alfonzo singing 'Soave sia il vento' from 'Così fan tutte'. The voices blend and interweave effortlessly. The women's voices float high and then hold their notes, suspended. They hold and float together, as if they were never going to end, and the bass voice climbs up and up and up beneath them … it is too much. Maestro abruptly turns away into the thick of the trees.

He comes to a clearing and sees a pretty young woman, a

girl, sitting on a bench, reading. A letter, it seems. And she is intent, mouthing the words. He watches her, admiring the fineness of her cheek and jaw, and hears, just faintly to start with, the Countess asking, 'Dove sono i bei momenti di dolcezza e di piacer?' from 'Le nozze di Figaro'. Wolfgang holds still as if in a trance. Tears well in his eyes and he turns and flees towards his house.

But the music follows him as he runs. He reaches the French doors, yanks them open, and slams them closed behind him. The voice and music abruptly stop.

He stands with his back to the windows, panting, then crosses to the piano and sits. He stares at the keys. He places one finger on the keyboard and strikes a note. He waits as if he is expecting something to happen. Nothing happens. He places the other fingers of the same hand on the keyboard and slowly, very slowly, plays the opening notes from Haydn's 'Capriccio Fantasia in C major'. He stops. And waits. Then suddenly he attacks the piano, in a tumult, in a frenzy, playing faster and faster, until blood starts welling up and pumping through the bandages of his hands. He reaches a climax, crashes his hands down violently on the keyboard, and lifts them again, frozen, in the air, after the last chord, and watches passively as drops of blood spatter down onto the keys, first just the white notes, then the black notes.

Part Five

EIGHTEEN

Italy

Teatro Municipale. Ferrara

Twenty-year-old Gioacchino Rossini is sitting half-way back in the empty seats of the Teatro Municipale auditorium, his head in his hands. Next to him is the theatre Impresario, Signor Saivelli. On the stage is seconda donna, Anna Saivelli. Anna is singing an aria from Gioacchino's latest opera, "Ciro in Babilonia" and singing it so badly that Gioacchino raises his arms in entreaty to God, muttering, "O Dio, Dio!" to himself. He stands as if he is about to intervene, then sits again.

"Please, do not upset yourself, Maestro Gioacchino," says Impresario Saivelli. "There are two whole days before opening night. I know my Anna will be perfectly adequate once she has learnt the notes."

"Two whole days!" rants Gioacchino, "Two whole days! She could spend two whole lifetimes and your Anna would not be adequate. She cannot sing!"

"May I remind you, sir, that …"

"No, you may not! Leave me! Leave me to my misery!"

The Impresario huffs, then exits slowly, leaving Gioacchino and his Anna alone together.

And a voice comes from out of the dark, from behind Gioacchino, "What a lump of a girl she is too!"

Startled, Gioacchino turns and peers into the gloom. He can dimly make out a cloaked figure in the back row of the auditorium, "What did you say, sir?"

"I said," says the figure, not moving, but enunciating clearly so that Gioacchino has no difficulty hearing above the noise coming from the stage, "... not only does she sing very badly, but she's also built like a plum pudding."

"This is true," concedes Gioacchino. "It takes rare talent to be this fat and this vile."

The figure laughs and moves forward. "Then why have her in the opera?"

"Because she's only singing the aria del sorbetto – while the audience is getting drinks and sherbet – because it's almost opening night – and because she's the Impresario's daughter and comes free with the theatre. Is that enough?"

"But she's as round as a panettone."

"I know! I know! But there's nothing I can do about that. Blame her mother, not me!"

"As for her singing ..."

"She will ruin me. Once they hear her, they won't come back in – they'll stay outside and eat sherbet."

"Except ..." The man pauses.

"Except what?"

"… she does have one note."

"One note?"

"Her middle B flat – listen …"

Gioacchino turns and listens. And sure enough, he hears it – a middle B flat that is tolerable. Almost good. Like a strawberry dropped into the middle of a pile of cow dung.

"You are right – it's bearable."

"So why don't you …?" and the figure stops again, "… no, you wouldn't dare."

"Wouldn't dare what?"

"Why don't you re-write the aria so that she has only the one note…?"

"… the B flat …"

"… the B flat, and give the orchestra the melody and the variations? Problem is – can you do it in time?"

"Do it in time? Of course I can do it in time! You are talking to Gioacchino Antonio Rossini, my friend!" and he picks up pen and paper and starts scribbling furiously.

It is opening night. The plum pudding, seconda donna, Anna Saivelli, is singing her new, one note, sherbet aria – "Chi disprezza gl'infelici". The audience in the theatre and foyer, gradually quietens their buying and jostling and gossiping and eating, and stops to listen, realizing something unusual is happening. Some return to the theatre, sherbet in hand. As the panettone, seconda donna, Anna Saivelli, finishes, they burst into spontaneous applause. The seconda donna is overwhelmed with surprise and delight, and takes an unscheduled bow, stopping the orchestra and the opera. The conductor joins in the applause and claps.

At the rear of the theatre, Maestro embraces Gioacchino. "Bravo! Bravo, maestro!"

Gioacchino is beside himself with joy. He returns the embrace with vigour. "It is you who is the maestro, my friend! I do not ask your name. You are Maestro! And I will never call you anything else, my friend, till the day I die!"

In the centre of a table sits a large confectionery ship, made of marzipan and cream. The ship lies on its side, its mast broken, its sails tattered, in an ocean of cream.

"My friends!" cries Gioacchino. "Here you have the good ship 'Ciro', our celebrated opera that you gloriously sang this night. It is, as you see, cast upon its side, doomed to sink, according to the reviewers, beneath the waves of history, but now, it is made famous forever, this very same night, by our celebrated one-note soprano, Anna Saivelli!"

And in the midst of the raucous and ribald applause, Anna blushes.

Gioacchino beckons her to move forward to the table. She does so, seemingly shy, but in reality, absolutely, overwhelmingly, delighted.

"Anna," cries Gioacchino over the din, "would you do us the honour of taking the first mouthful of the good cake Ciro?"

Anna beams and leans over the cake, reaching for a knife, and Gioacchino suddenly presses her head forward and down so that it is buried in the marzipan and cream. There are roars of disbelief and delight from all assembled. Maestro emits a baying laugh which is lost in the din.

Anna lifts her face from the cake. The marzipan and cream are in her hair, in her eyes, up her nostrils.

Gioacchino leans in close and licks her cheek. He swallows, smacks his lips, then licks her forehead. "My dear One-Note Anna," he cries for all to hear, "you look divine – and taste even better!"

Anna One-note blinks at him through the haze of cake and cream. She does not move. The room quickly goes quiet. Her tongue creeps out of her mouth and curls to lick her lower lip, most lasciviously, then, with her fingers, she scoops cream and marzipan from her chin and stuffs her fingers into her mouth. She opens her mouth wide, showing teeth and cream and tongue and marzipan, and breaks into a cavernous grin, which acts as a signal for the company to dive into the cake and the cream, and devour it.

Gioacchino leans back in his chair and closes his eyes. He takes out a handkerchief from his breast pocket and wipes his forehead, and is immediately standing side-stage in the Teatro del Corso. Isabella is thrusting her hand out towards him, and holding it there, urging him. Gioacchino reaches for her hand, kissing it and placing it on his heart, then slowly sliding it down to his crotch.

There is a scream of delight from One-Note Anna as someone slips his hand, with cream and marzipan, down the back of her dress and onto her buttocks.

Gioacchino's eyes fly open, startled, and he sits bolt up-right.

"You live dangerously, my friend," says Maestro. Maestro is nursing a glass of wine and sitting opposite Gioacchino. The party is in full swing behind him.

"Why do you say that?"

"Because you dare to write a one-note aria, because you risk the panettone's fury by burying her face in the cake, and because you wrote an opera in which two women are seen to be lovers."

"What? Oh, you mean "L'Equivoco"! But it only played three times before the police closed it down."

"I saw it."

"Did you? And what else have you seen?"

"Everything you've written since you were fourteen years old."

Gioacchino leans forward, suddenly intrigued. "My God! Then you're either a fool or a pervert!"

"Neither – unless you class liking your women big as perverted. And when I say big, I mean, vast, enormous, colossal! You see, my friend, I have a secret – something only my wife knows – I have a weakness for arses – and I mean women's arses, of course. When I close my eyes, I dream of mounds, sitting there, snug, together. Like breasts – only bigger and better. 'Arse' – just say the word – taste it – roll your tongue around it …"

"Arse …" says Gioacchino, "Arse … arse … yes, it does have a ring to it …"

And they both roar with laughter.

"But it's got to be prime arse – none of your little maiden bums for me …" Maestro stops. "Am I shocking you?"

"No!" cries Gioacchino. "I can see them! I can feel them! Go on!"

"One day," says Maestro, "I'll write a concerto to the female arse – a concerto for tuba perhaps …"

"Or double bass!"

"Why don't we write it together?" says Maestro.

"Why not?"

"Then we will – but first you must finish what you're currently writing."

Gioacchino pauses and stares at Maestro. "How do you know I'm writing something at the moment?"

"Because you're penniless."

"And how do you know that?"

"Because you're a composer, and all composers are penniless. It's a rule – to be a composer you have to have an empty belly and a bare arse." Maestro stands, turns, pulls down his breeches and exposes his bare arse.

Gioacchino convulses with laughter, tears in his eyes. "I'm … I'm working on an opera called Demetrio and Polibio, at the moment," he says, "and I've just written a quartet – such a quartet! Would you like to see it?"

"See it? You have it with you?"

"Of course I have it with me." He pulls a manuscript out from his shirt. "I work everywhere – sometimes when I'm shitting I get my best ideas. They just seem to force their way out." And Gioacchino bursts into laughter again.

Maestro takes the proffered manuscript, reads it quickly, then looks up at Gioacchino.

"It is sublime! It has such a lightness of touch. It has grace. A freshness of the morning ... may I be so bold as to make a little suggestion?"

"Suggest away, my friend."

"Don't end it."

"Don't end it?"

"It's too beautiful to end ..." and he plays an imaginary piano and sings, "dum, dum! No – hold these notes here ..." and he stabs a finger down on the score, "like an outcry of voices, hanging, suspended ..."

Part Six

NINETEEN

Italy

Gioacchino's rooms. Ferrara

Gioacchino is lying in the bath. He is writing music with a quill on a sheet of manuscript. Gioacchino is not alone in the bath. One-Note Anna Saivelli fills the other end to overflowing. She is soaping his foot, using her breasts as if they were giant sponges, while he writes. Suddenly he points his quill at her, "Sing! The B flat …"

And Anna sings her one note.

"Perfetto!" he exclaims, and throws the manuscript and quill to the far wall.

Anna stretches out her own foot to touch him. Gioacchino takes hold of her foot and pulls. She disappears under the water. A tidal wave cascades onto the floor.

Gioacchino stands. "And now," he announces, "I go to Milan."

Anna surfaces, spluttering, "Milan? Why do you go to Milan?"

"To see her," he says and he steps out of the bath, dripping water onto the floor.

"Her? Who is her?"

"'Who is her?' 'Who is her?' You do not refer to her as a 'her.' She is Isabella! My Isabella!"

And with enormous dignity, the nude and still dripping Gioacchino walks out the door.

TWENTY

Italy

La Scala. Milan

Isabella Colbran, prima donna, takes her bows, to rapturous applause as another performance of Nicolini's 'Coriolano' ends. She is resplendent in a dress of feathers and sweeping silk train. And little else.

Doves and canaries are released from theatre boxes into the auditorium, and fly and flutter and shit everywhere. The hubbub from the audience multiplies. Isabella bows low and her breasts balloon dangerously, to the delight of the audience.

Gioacchino, holding a huge bunch of flowers, is standing in the front row, applauding louder and more enthusiastically than anyone else. And, in a fit of enthusiasm and madness, he climbs onto the orchestra barrier and leaps across the orchestra pit onto the stage. Almost. He teeters on the edge of the stage and the orchestra pit for two, three, seconds, and valiantly throws the flowers towards Isabella. They miss and are caught by the gay countertenor. The counter tenor blows Gioacchino a kiss just as Gioacchino disappears into the orchestra pit and crashes onto the cellos and double basses below.

The cast and audience erupt anew in applause and laughter.

When Gioacchino eventually disentangles himself from the instruments, fights off two cello players and one double bass player, and looks up at the stage, Isabella has gone.

TWENTY-ONE

Italy

Gioacchino's rooms. Ferrara

Maestro is seated at the keyboard, playing the "Di tanti palpiti … Mi rivedrai, ti rivedrò …" refrain from Gioacchino's, and his, upcoming opera 'Tancredi'.

Gioacchino is lying on top of the piano, full length, manuscript and quill pen in his hands. "You know what, Maestro? This opera reminds me of something … something I've seen and heard …"

Maestro stops playing in mid-phrase and waits, poised, for Gioacchino to continue.

"I don't mean the music so much – it's more the ideas – full of opposites, don't you think? I mean – romance and foolishness, affection and affectation, stupidity, charm … it reminds me … it reminds me of…"

"Of Così …"

"… fan tutte! Yes, that's it! Our old friend, Mozart. Have you ever seen it?"

"Once or twice, many years ago now. What about you?"

One Note Anna has come in with a tray of cream cake fingers – she has one sticking out of her mouth – and has climbed on top of the piano, next to Gioacchino. She inserts a cream cake finger into his mouth.

"I was hungry," says Anna. "Your Tancredi can wait a little while longer." She extends a cream finger towards Maestro. Maestro reaches and takes it. "You've got a whole week to finish …" She stops and stares at Maestro's hands. "How … whatever happened to your hands?"

Maestro drops his hands immediately. "An accident, some years ago. I've forgotten how I …"

There is a loud knocking on the street door.

Gioacchino climbs off the piano, goes to the door and opens it.

A splendidly dressed, bows and feathers, hair-coiffured, strikingly good-looking, clearly aristocratic, but slightly past her best woman, bursts into the room. Her hands are full of bags and hat boxes. She drops the bags and boxes and throws herself into Gioacchino's arms.

"I've left him!" she declares. "I couldn't pretend any longer! The man is a pig! A boor! I mean, when I told him that I loved you and wanted to leave him, he said 'Go then' and threw me out! Can you believe it? So, I've come to live with you, darling Gioacchino. Isn't that lovely?"

She looks at his face to read his reaction to the news and, for the first time, is aware of the cream cake finger sticking out of his mouth, and that there are other people in the room. She looks from one to the other and then back to Gioacchino. She sighs and strokes his face.

Gioacchino gulps in the last of the cream cake finger, releases himself from her embrace, with some difficulty, and turns in circles trying to look at everyone, all at the same time.

"Yes ... yes!" he says – but it was more of a squeak really. "How lovely! Well, here's a to-do in anybody's book. Yes. Well ... oh, I do apologise! What manners! You haven't met, have you? No, of course you haven't. This is One Note ... sorry ... this is Anna Saivelli, this is my friend, Maestro, and you are ... I'm sorry but I've ..." and he rushes to Maestro's side, grabs hold of his arm and pulls him towards the door. "Sorry! We have to leave immediately, I'm afraid. Urgent business. Sorry, ladies. Can't stay!"

And he is gone, dragging Maestro with him.

Both women stare at the closed door, then turn and face one another, and smile.

TWENTY-TWO

Italy

La Scala. Milan

Pacuvio is singing the jangling, verbal nonsense aria, from Gioacchino's, and Maestro's, "Tancredi". He comes to the refrain, "Di tanti palpiti … Mi rivedrai, ti rivedrò…" and the audience erupts. Some sing along with him, some dance along with him. And when it is done, they demand he do it again. Gioacchino, at the keyboard, nods to Pacuvio, and the jamboree begins anew.

After the crowds disperse, Maestro and Gioacchino escape to a nearby ristorante. Maestro does not like crowds, he says, especially opera crowds, he says, especially Italian opera crowds.

"Why?" asks Gioacchino.

"Because they are opinionated," says Maestro. "They interrupt. They can take an opera and a composer to their hearts with such passion that they can elevate it and him to the level of kings and popes, and then just as quickly, and just as passionately, especially if money changes hands, they can destroy it and him."

"True! True!" cries Gioacchino.

"Italians are corrupt", says Maestro, winding up in his story-telling. "It is in their nature. An Italian will feed you and embrace you and be your undying friend, with such grace, such charm, such passion, and then he will cheat you, sell you, even kill you. Because that is the Italian way!"

And Gioacchino, being an Italian, agrees whole-heartedly and, being an Italian, tucks, just as whole-heartedly, into his steak with paté foie gras, dash of Madeira, butter, flour, bouillon, and mushrooms, his own recipe delivered days before, and cooked to perfection by the chef.

Over a mouthful, Gioacchino says he will accept the burden of adulation, while it lasts, for both of them. It will be hard but he will do it. He is happy for Maestro to stay out of the limelight, if that is his choosing. As long as they share the profits, Gioacchino says, graciously, he will suffer on the cross of fame for both of them. And they laugh uproariously, both happy, both content.

There are four people seated at the next table, staring at them. Two men and two women. Dressed for a night at the opera. And one of them, a man, at their laughter, leaps to his feet, raises his glass, spilling some over his female companion, and sings, full voice, very badly but very enthusiastically, "Di tanti palpiti ... Mi rivedrai, ti rivedrò ...", and toasts "Gioacchino Rossini!" His companions surge to their feet and join his raucous rendition.

Maestro turns away but Gioacchino raises his glass to them. "Alla salute!" he calls and tosses back his wine.

"Alla salute!" they echo, toss back their glasses, and sit and laugh and chatter, very pleased with themselves indeed.

When things are quiet again, Maestro leans across to Gioacchino, "You are becoming famous, my friend."

"So it seems – but fame does not fill your pocket."

"I know, I know."

"But commissions will – come with me to Venice, Maestro."

"Venice? Why Venice?"

"Because I have received commissions to write two more operas there this year – and, more importantly, it will be the season of the Carnivale in Venice – the time of masks and intrigue and secret love affairs."

"I have a wife."

"Bring her too!"

"She cannot … will not … come. She was injured … disfigured, some years ago and is now reluctant to appear in public. I will speak with her, and if she is content, I will follow you to Venice."

Gioacchino raises his glass again. "To masks, intrigue and secret love affairs!"

"… to masks and intrigue!" says Maestro.

And they drink.

Later, as they leave, and pass the neighbours' table, Gioacchino dances a few steps and breaks into "Mi rivedrai, ti rivedrò …"

His new friends leap to their feet and join him.

Maestro has already gone.

TWENTY-THREE

Italy

Pianoro

Magdalena looks down into a blazing fire. A log collapses and tumbles, sending up a flare of hot sparks and ashes. She does not move. Maestro paces nervously, waiting for her to speak. She says nothing. He moves close to her and puts his hand on her shoulder. Slowly, almost reluctantly, she turns and faces him.

"You are playing a very dangerous game, my love," she says quietly.

"Those are almost the exact words I used to Gioacchino, just a few days ago!" exclaims Maestro.

Magdalena is not to be deflected. "Gioacchino Rossini is recognized wherever he goes – people whistle his tunes in the street – they queue for hours to get into his operas – and the man has written five operas in a year!"

"Yes, we have, and we have earned good commissions for each of them."

"There you go again!" she cries. "That is precisely what I am talking about! People are already saying that it is impossible for one man, on his own, to write what he has written. There is rumour. There is gossip …"

"There is always rumour and gossip …"

"Not like this! It's not as if we need the money – van Swieten saw to that."

"He left the money to you – not to me!"

"Because you would have spent it all within a year!"

She moves to Maestro and takes his hands. "My love, you are seen with him. It is only a matter of time before someone recognizes you, and then where will we be?"

"Lena, I go everywhere cloaked and shrouded. I've worn beards. I've worn wigs. And I've been dead now for over twenty years. Who is going to recognise me?"

"But he has become the toast of Italy! How do you bear the praise when it all goes to him and none to you?"

"Because I must! I am alive again. I live through him. Don't deny me that! It is bad enough not to write in my own name – but not to write at all? I would rather die!"

Magdalena buries her face in his shoulder.

"Now that I have found him, I will not give him up."

And she cries.

Maestro strokes her hair and kisses her head. "If there is risk, I accept it. If there is danger, then I will live dangerously." He puts his hands on her face and turns it up to his. "I will go to Venice – and I will wear a mask at all times – even when I'm in the bath or straining on the commode. Will that satisfy you?"

In spite of herself, Magdalena begins to laugh.

Maestro hugs her to him. "Let's not waste any more time, my love. Let's to bed."

TWENTY-FOUR

Italy

A room in Venice

Maestro is seated at the keyboard. He hears a noise in the corridor outside and quickly pulls his Venetian mask down over his face.

Gioacchino throws open the door, stands in the doorway and snarls to the room, "I hate the little shit!"

Maestro lifts the mask up so that it sits like a plate on top of his head, "Who?"

"Cera, that bastard Impresario at Teatro San Moise! He's cheating me again. Do you know what he paid me for "L'Inganno" back in January?"

"No, what?"

"Two hundred and fifty francs."

"Francs are better than lire."

"That's not the point, dammit!" he screams. "Francs or poxy lire – who cares? I'm worth a lot more than what that shit gave me!"

Maestro hurriedly pulls the mask down over his face again, "Right!

Right! The little shit!"

"And now he's trying it again. He hates me because I accepted a commission from La Fenice. I'm working with his enemy, he says, and only the enemy of his enemy would be his friend, he says. So now he won't even pay me the two hundred and fifty francs he paid me last time! He's talking two hundred francs. Can you believe it?"

"The shit!" says Maestro, and lifts the mask up again. "Then pay him back in kind."

"What do you mean?"

"If he is cheating you, then cheat him."

"How?"

"Write him a two hundred franc opera."

"Aah!" cries Gioacchino, and tears off his topcoat, his scarf and his hat and throws them onto the floor in front of him and stamps on them, in a fit, in a tantrum, jumping up and down with much fury and considerable pleasure. "I can't deliberately write something cheap and nasty just to spite him! I'd have to live with it afterwards!"

"Calm! Calm yourself, dear friend! I am not talking about writing inferior music or an inferior story. Your name will be unblemished. I'm talking about his production. Write him a two hundred franc disaster. Make sure the production is full of outrageous extravagances and tricks that will guarantee to offend the audience – and lose him whole satchels of francs."

"Such as what?"

"Such as ..." and Maestro stops and smiles indulgently at Gioacchino, "... but before I say another word, you must promise to go back to him now, before it opens, and accept his two hundred francs –

on condition that he pays you beforehand!"

"I will! Now, what are you suggesting?"

"What is the top note of your bass, Ravelli, in the opera?"

"An 'F'."

"Then we'll write him in a string of 'G's'. What is the lowest note of your soprano?"

"Um … a 'B' – don't tell me! – we give her some beautiful bottom 'A's and 'G's!"

"As for the violins …"

The orchestra of the Teatro San Moise is playing the overture to Rossini's "Il Signor Bruschino". When they reach the allegro movement, the violinists begin striking the backs of their bows rhythmically against the tin covers of the candle-lit music stands in front of them, producing a metallic, tin-can, pizzicato effect. Two stands fall over, causing a minor panic, flurry of arms, legs, music sheets, and a fire. The audience listens in stunned silence, then, as the striking continues, being an Italian audience, they start booing, then calling out and whistling. Another candle falls onto the foot of a cellist who kicks it, sending it skittering back at the offending violinist. A fight ensues.

Cera, the impresario, hurries from the back of the theatre down to the orchestra pit, in consternation, and in doing so passes Gioacchino, who is sitting at the keyboard, grinning from ear to ear.

TWENTY-FIVE

Italy

Gioacchino's and Maestro's room. Venice

Maestro and Gioacchino are sitting up in their respective single beds at each end of the bedroom. It is night. It is freezing cold. Both have wrapped blankets around their shoulders and are wearing woollen hats, with flaps, and fingerless gloves, to keep warm. Each has a quill pen and sheets of manuscript in his hands and an inkpot on his side table. They are composing.

Maestro stretches out his hand to his side table and lifts up a withered poppy. He picks out the poppy heads one by one, pierces them with a needle and then drops them into a small glazed crock of wine on the side table. He picks up a second, similar crock alongside it, and puts it to his lips.

"Joining me?" he asks.

Gioacchino shakes his head. "No, no, thank you. That concoction will kill you in the end, my friend."

Maestro empties the crock, "Something usually does," he says, "but a soupcon of laudanum makes the waiting for it to happen much more pleasant, I find, now … Mustapha sings to his love …" He looks up at Gioacchino, "… how shall we name her?"

"Isabella."

"Isabella? But isn't that a Spanish name? Surely we need an obviously Italian name for this opera?"

"Isabella."

"What about Maria or Anna perhaps – after your mother?"

"Isabella! Isabella! Isabella!"

"Right, Isabella it is then. Lovely name. Now, where is that delightful little tune you wrote for Mustapha last night? I saw it somewhere …"

"In my coat. Over there, hanging on the door."

Maestro waits for Gioacchino to get out of bed and fetch it. Gioacchino does not move. "Well?" says Maestro.

"Well what?"

"Aren't you going to get it? We need to finish the scene."

"No. Too cold to get out of bed. You get it."

"Me get it? An old crock like me, get out of bed in the middle of a freezing, damp, Venetian night? Out of the question, my friend. My balls are like ice. They'll drop off. You do it. Go on. Your balls are much younger than mine."

"Younger, yes – but more worn and used than yours! And, I need mine more!" He roars with laughter.

After a slight pause, Maestro laughs too.

"Look, forget last night's tune," says Gioacchino. "I'll write another."

"Write another? Rather than get out of bed and get your little testicles cold – you'll write another!"

"Yes," says Gioacchino, "and it'll be better – give me a shopping list and I'll turn it into an aria. Just watch." And he scribbles furiously with his quill – spraying ink onto the blanket.

"Right!" cries Maestro, and he scribbles furiously also, "And I'll accompany Mustapha's throbbing heart with a quivering violin … can you feel the trembling?"

"Two violins – playing octaves!" says Gioacchino, scribbling even faster, "… and from below, deep down below…"

"… his throbbing breast begins to swell …"

"… there erupts, a rigid, upright bassoon," gasps Gioacchino, and he thrusts his arm to the ceiling, out of control "… till it bursts in a climax, a crescendo of …"

"Stop!" cries Gioacchino.

Maestro stops still in frozen surprise, quill poised in the air.

"I have a confession to make," says Gioacchino.

"A confession?" says Maestro, hand still poised. "What confession?"

"I can contain myself no longer." He turns and faces Maestro.

"We must leave for Naples the moment we finish our 'L'italiana in Algeri'.

"For Naples?"

"Yes, we must leave the moment the last note is written…"

"Naples is a very long way from Venice, Gioacchino."

"… to go to her."

"Her?"

"Isabella."

"Isabella who?"

"Isabella who makes my mouth water when I say her name, Isabella who smells of the earth and incense and hidden promise, Isabella who makes me sweat and tremble just at the thought of holding her ... of touching her ..." He pulls out the handkerchief from under his nightshirt and wafts it in the air. "Dear God, smell that!" He puts it to his own nose and inhales deeply. "Aah ... here are her armpits ..." he inhales again, "here is the valley between her breasts ..." inhaling again, "... her neck, her mouth ..." inhaling again, "I've never washed it – not in six – no seven years. Isabella!"

"I see. That Isabella. Wait a minute – is this the same Isabella you charged off to Milan to see?

"Yes."

"And you saw her ...?"

"Yes."

"And what did she say to you?"

"She didn't speak to me."

"She didn't speak to you?"

"No."

"Why not?"

"She was busy."

"Busy! She was too busy to see the famous, the handsome, the up-and-coming composer, Gioacchino Rossini? My friend, I'd forget all about this toffee-nosed, two-bit soprano of yours, if I were you. She's obviously not worthy of…"

"You don't understand – I had … an accident."

"An accident? What kind of accident?"

"A … musical accident."

"A musical … accident?"

"Basta! Basta! Basta!" screams Gioacchino. "You're not my mother! We're going to Naples!"

"Yes! Fine, fine, my friend," says Maestro so sweetly that he is almost sick. "Naples and Isabella it is then."

TWENTY-SIX

Italy

Venice to Naples

They embark on a carrack in the port of Venice, destined for Bologna. The boat is more a ballinger than a carrack really – a smaller, sea-going vessel, distinguished by its lack of a forecastle, carrying a sail extended on a sprit, less than a hundred tons, and with a shallow draught, which was essential, given the coastal waters they are to travel. The Venetian lagoon stretches fifty kilometres, north to south, and accesses the open sea via a bar.

Gioacchino and Maestro pay for a cabin, which is actually a share of one of the two cabins on board, along with three other passengers. The price includes lodging, meaning a space to sleep under cover during the night, and dinner, meaning bread, a round of cheese, and rough red wine, which is plentiful. They drink copious amounts of the cheap wine, chatter with their companions while they negotiate the lagoon, and attempt to go to sleep, but are soon out on deck, over the deck-rails, heaving up the wine, bread and cheese into the Venetian lagoon, just moments after they leave the lagoon and hit the open sea.

And, the following morning, when they have recovered enough, they talk Elisabetta. Elisabetta, Queen of England, because that is the only thing that Gioacchino wants to talk about. And write about. And sing and compose about. He has even brought writing materials and a copy of Schmidt's libretto, based on Federici's play of the year before.

"I name you Gioacchino The Organized!" cries Maestro, surprised and impressed.

"As our friend Aristotle said, one swallow does not a summer make," says Gioacchino. "I am as likely to forget to change my breeches tomorrow. Which I might do today actually – I suffered a little spillage, last night, I'm afraid. Now, where are my breeches?"

"You are wearing them, my friend."

"These are the only breeches I have? Are you saying there are no spares packed in our luggage?"

"No, my friend. You were in such a tearing hurry to get to Naples, to your Isabella, you forgot to pack almost everything – except your dress coat – and obviously your writing materials, it seems. So, no spare breeches," and Maestro can barely hold his laughter.

"But the journey to Naples will take seven days! You'll have to lend me a pair of yours. You did pack some, I hope."

"I did – but there lies a little problem, Gioacchino – a problem size. We differ significantly in height and in girth, my friend!" and he can no longer control himself and roars with laughter.

"Enough! Enough! No more talk of breeches!" cries Gioacchino. He grabs a scroll of manuscript and a quill, and says, quiet and serious, "We will open Elisabetta on a duet between Leicester and his young wife, Matilde, whom he has secretly married, and introduced to the royal court, dressed as a page boy! In a minor key, I suggest."

"A piece of genius, my friend! Elisabetta will be furious! So, perhaps a staccato rush of orders from her, followed by silence, then…"

"Yes! Yes!" breathes Gioacchino, and they are both soon lost in writing the music: Gioacchino the duet, Maestro the staccato orders, the silence, and the queenly aria to follow.

Their boat reaches the estuary that leads to the mouth of the River Po, sail into the river and then heave-to. Two men in two small boats, on either side of the river, row out to their vessel, each dragging a sturdy rope behind them. The ropes are attached to the vessel. On the other end of the ropes are horses, who now take up the slack and slowly but steadily tow the vessel up-river.

And they arrive in Bologna. Actually, they skirt Bologna, as Gioacchino has no wish to waste time on Bolognese distractions. Especially as they are told repeatedly by agitated citizens of Bologna, that since the fall of Napoleon, the Congress of Vienna had, only months before, placed Bologna back under the oppressive and hated rule of the Papal States. And that's where they are going, of course. Which is not good news, again according to everybody they talked to – "The roads are unsafe!" they said. "There are cut-throat bandits all along the notorious Appian way from Rome to Naples! From Terracina to Fondi! They hide in the bushes and leap out at lone horsemen and at carriages! No one is safe!"
"So, what do we do?" they ask.

"Travel in large numbers," says one.

"Hire guards to escort you," says another.

"Sometimes the guards are worse than the bandits!" says yet

another. "They lead you safely out of the city, then slit your throat once they are in the woods, then come back looking for more trusting idiots!"

In the end, they find a carriage of priests and clerics who have banded together for the leg to Rome, where they stay in a filthy inn on the outskirts of the city, don't sleep in the beds because they are infested with vermin and other unspeakables, and then, the next day, are fortunate to be able to join three carriages travelling together for safety along the Appian Way. Their carriage holds four, with three more on top, hanging on to the outside rigging. The other two inside are sullen and clearly apprehensive, so Maestro and Gioacchino ignore them, deposit their possessions above and below the seats, stuffing bread and wine inside pockets, and busy themselves with Elisabetta, Gioacchino rendering a powerful version of Norfolk's citation of Leicester's treachery to the Queen, with tremolo strings and scurrying pizzicato, while Maestro is focusing on Leicester's prison scene with its dream sequence via a fractured vocal line and wind obligatos. Happy as boys – even though one of them is twenty-three-years old and the other sixty-two, ankle-deep in mud.

They have a minor disagreement at one point as they pass over a very rickety bridge south of Rome, when they swap manuscripts and read the other's work. Maestro comments that Gioacchino's arias for the Queen are decidedly coloratura in voice range, which will demand brilliant technique, but all Gioacchino will say is, "Trust me."

So he does.

They reach Terracina, late one afternoon, and seek out a beddable inn, because they are exhausted. They have slept little in the carriage, and barely more in the inns on the way. And they are successful. The inn is clean, the beds are vermin-free, and Gioacchino pays the host immediately to secure the board.

And Fabio invites them to eat. They sit on forms at a board cum table. Fabio sits with them. Fabio is an unusually large man with massive arms and shoulders, as if he were a wrestler. He deposits a large pitcher of wine in the centre of the board, pours three cups without prompting and raises one in a toast, "Buona salute!"

They drink to his health, to their health, to the health of everyone in the carriages, to the citizens of Terracina – except the bandits of course – and Fabio refills the pitcher from a barrel. His wife serves Pappa al pomodoro in trenchers of bread. They drink the soup from the trenchers, then eat the trenchers. The wife sets a bowl of fagioli all'uccelletto in front of them and they dip their spoons into the bowl, scoop up the beans until the bowl is empty. This is followed by pollo arosto, with the chicken plucked from the spit that sits over the fire that burns in the same room they are eating in, and torn apart on the board in front of them. Fabio refills the pitcher. It is a meal fit for kings. Peasant kings perhaps, but kings nevertheless. Simple, well-cooked, delicious.

"This is Italy," says Gioacchino.

Fabio tells them what is to come the next day and the days that will follow. "We are on the edge of the most notorious stretch road known to man," he says. "… the Appian Way from Terracina, the last town in the Papal Territories, to Fondi, the first town in the Neapolitan dominions. This is where the bandits live, my friends. Once you leave my house, you step into their house. If you reach Fondi, you will be safe."

"Why? Why will we be safe?" asks Maestro.

"Because the King of Naples pays farmers to burn the bushes and trees on either side of the road, to give carriages a better view ahead, so they can be warned of danger." He takes another huge gulp of wine and smacks his lips as if it were his first. "And, the king stations soldiers – every quarter of an hour – every two kilometres – and, if they catch lo banditi, they are hanged on the spot."

All three touch cups. "Salute del Re!"

The next morning, on the carriage lumbering south, Gioacchino and Maestro are deep into Elisabetta again. But every now and then, one will poke his head out of a carriage door and peer nervously ahead.

TWENTY-SEVEN

Italy

Teatro San Carlo. Naples

Gioacchino and Maestro bribe their way into Teatro San Carlo, the largest theatre in Naples, indeed, in Italy, seating two thousand five hundred souls, including one hundred and eighty-four boxes. They make their way into the wings and as soon as they get sight of the stage, Gioacchino stops dead in his tracks, and stares. On the stage is a truly Junoesque female form, side-on, with jutting breasts, strapped-in waist, and truly gibbous buttocks, as she bends over to touch her feet. It is a rare sight.

"Isabella!" breathes Gioacchino.

"Oh, the arse on her!" whispers Maestro, "Not big enough for me, mind you," he adds quickly, "but give her a few years ..."

Gioacchino immediately moves onto the stage, towards her, when suddenly, from the other side of the stage, a burly, powerful figure of a man, with bulbous nose and startling blue eyes, sweeps on, followed by a quivering man carrying – more juggling – a roll of manuscript, quill, and ink in a pot.

"Darling!" he cries, and he holds his arms out towards Isabella to embrace her.

"Domenico," she gushes, and accepts his embrace by pressing his face down between her breasts. He lingers there for some seconds, then drops an arm to her waist and sweeps her off across the stage, closely followed by his juggling secretary.

They pass within inches of Gioacchino and Maestro, without seeing them.

"They are together!" says Gioacchino, breathless in disbelief.

"The princess and the frog," says Maestro.

"How can she?"

"Because he's a very rich and powerful frog, I'd say."

"Perhaps when she kisses him, he will turn into a prince."

"I'm sure she's already kissed him, Gioacchino, and he's still a frog. In fact, I'd go so far as to say that she's already…"

"Don't say it! Don't you dare say it!" gasps Gioacchino. "Not a word, I warn you, or I will kill you, then I will kill myself."

"My friend, may I say something?"

"If you must."

"She is… how do I say this? She is somewhat… larger and taller than you."

"Yes, so much beauty needs a generous canvas to be fully appreciated."

"And… she is a little older than you."

"Of course she is! She is a woman, not a girl."

"Then why not let an older man approach her on your behalf? If you like, I will meet with her, talk with her, extol your virtues to her – tell her how well endowed you are."

"You think so?"

"Well, you are, aren't you?"

"Yes, I am."

"There you are then."

TWENTY-EIGHT

Italy

Isabella's drawing room. Naples

Isabella is bathing in a high-backed hip bath. She is attended by her maid, Gabriella. Gabriella is tying up her mistress' hair so that it exposes her long, beautiful neck, the line of her shoulders, the softness of her skin – and to keep her hair out of the water, of course. If visitors arrive, as visitors often do for her bath – costumiers, jewellers, artists, admirers … then she is ready.

There is a knock at the door. The bath is side-on to the door and Isabella adjusts her profile, then nods to Gabriella. Gabriella opens the door.

There is a little man wearing a pink wig waiting at the door. Maestro. He enters before he is invited and sweeps low in a fulsome bow.

Isabella takes a towel from Gabriella and partially covers her breasts. It is not easy. It is a small towel.

Maestro steps forward to get an even better view. "If may be so bold, my lady, but I was hoping I could take just a moment of your time?"

"What is it about?" says Isabella, clearly not particularly interested or impressed by such a small, unknown, and definitely older man.

"Something to your advantage, I assure you, my lady."

"I am not 'your lady', my friend … ah well, a brief moment perhaps – but you must stay behind the bath – for decency's sake, sir."

Maestro takes one step to the side but retains his clear view of a dark brown, protuberant nipple – clearly intended, he decides.

"You have an admirer, my lady."

"Do I?"

"Yes, a great admirer – a truly talented composer, famous throughout Europe."

Isabella discards the towel and soaps her arms and shoulders. "Is he now?"

"And able, nay willing, nay desperately keen, my lady, to offer you leading roles in his up-coming operas."

Isabella turns full-on to look at him.

Maestro is hugely encouraged and a somewhat excited by this reaction. "If you like, I'll play you just a little …" And before she can stop him, he darts to the piano, sits and immediately begins playing, a medley of the themes from Gioacchino's recent operas.

Isabella is now fully front on from his new position, but she makes no effort to cover her nakedness or turn away.

As he plays, he jerks his head to signal Gabriella to leave the room.

Gabriella hesitates, looks at Isabella, but Isabella has closed her eyes, so Gabriella exits.

Maestro becomes more and more excited as he plays.

Isabella is clearly very impressed and astonished at the virtuosity of his playing. "Bravo! Bravo!" she cries.

And Maestro, who sees this as a clear signal of intimate encouragement and invitation, rushes from the keyboard towards Isabella and lunges at her, trying to embrace her.

"Sir!" screams Isabella.

"I adore you, Isabella!" he gasps and grapples with her wet, slippery and nude upper body.

"Get your filthy old hands off me, sir!" screams Isabella.

She stands and leaps out of the bath. The lunging Maestro is carried forward by his own momentum and falls headfirst into the water. His head emerges. He has lost his wig, his hair is plastered to his skull, and his clothes are sodden.

Isabella has snatched a gown from a chair and she clutches it to her bosoms. She stares at Maestro then bursts out laughing. She calls, "Gabriella! Come quick! Come and see the little drowned rat who says he adores me!"

Gabriella rushes in, and together they roar and roar with laughter as the drowned rat climbs, with great difficulty, out of the tub and stands in front of them, dripping. Gabriella darts forward, fishes his wig out of the water, and plants it on his head, back to front, then returns to Isabella's side so she can see.

The two women stand and admire Gabriella's work. Serious. It is a big decision.

"What do you think, my lady?"

"It suits him! Well done, Gabriella, but perhaps … perhaps a little more to the right?"

Gabriella darts back to Maestro, tips the wig fractionally more to the right and hurries back to Isabella's side.

"Yes," breathes Isabella, and they both burst out laughing.

Maestro exits hurriedly.

TWENTY-NINE

Italy

Teatro San Carlo. Naples

Isabella sweeps up the steps, enters the wings, sends two stage-hands who are carrying a wooden cloud, scurrying out of her way, and arrives on stage. She makes a beeline for Impresario Domenico Barbaja who is talking to a man she does not know. "Domenico," she announces so that he and everyone else in the theatre can hear, "I must have a larger room, I cannot put up with that hen-coop of a dressing room for a moment longer."

"Of course you can't, my dearest," toadies Domenico. "I will eject Strombelli immediately – we can always find another tenor, can't we?" and he roars with laughter at his own joke.

Isabella does not laugh.

"My dearest," gushes Domenico, "may I introduce you to Signor Gioacchino Rossini, the celebrated composer. Signor... Signorina Isabella Colbran!"

And Isabella is suddenly all charm, girlish even, as far as it was possible for a woman of her proportions to be. "Maestro Rossini!" she simpers, and she curtsies low and offers him her hand.

Her breasts swim before Gioacchino's eyes. He can see nothing else.

She stays low, looks up at him, and realizes immediately what he is staring at. She breathes in deeply, and waves her hand in the air to remind him that it's there.

Gioacchino grasps her hand, kisses it with fervour, and holds on to it.

She stands, and the breasts resume their proper place. She is so tall, so mature, so elegant, and he is so short and boy-like that they look, to everyone else on the stage, like mother and son, ready to go out for a play in the park. But they themselves seem completely unaware of any such disparity.

"I have heard so much about you, Signor. In fact, people seem to talk about nothing else these days. I mean, its Pietra this, Tancredi that – Ferrara, Bologna, Venice – and even, La Scala, I hear?"

"A trifling – you do me too great an honour, madame." And he kisses her hand again.

"Oh, I'm not a madame, my dear maestro – you make me sound like an old dame," she laughs and flutters an imaginary fan to hide her seeming embarrassment. "Diva will do, or, if you prefer… just plain, simple, Isabella."

"There is nothing plain or simple about you, Isabella," says her gushing gallant.

Isabella laughs again indulgently and is suddenly conscious of the fact that Gioacchino is still holding her hand, and she slowly, sinuously, and clearly reluctantly, disengages it. "And why are you in Naples, sir?"

"Impresario Domenico Barbaja here has asked me to write something for him."

"Domenico!" she squeals. "You sly devil you! You didn't tell me!" She turns back to Gioacchino and drops her voice into deep mezzo. "And what is this little something?"

"Elisabetta. Set in England."

"In England! And would there, by any chance, be a little role in it for me – just a teeny, weeny, little something?"

"I was thinking, no hoping … perhaps Elisabetta?"

"The Queen?" and it's a squeal again. "Oh, aren't you charming! Isn't he just charming, Domenico?"

"Charming," says Domenico, and he takes Isabella's arm as if to lead her off.

Gioacchino intervenes quickly and steps in front of her, "We have met once before, Isabella."

"Your face does look vaguely familiar … no, I'm sure I would recall such a face if we had."

"We met in Teatro del Corso, in Bologna."

"Did we? I don't …"

And Gioacchino pulls out the handkerchief from inside his shirt and dangles it in front of her.

She takes it and examines it. "This is my handkerchief – there, it has my letter "I" on it! How did you … oh, you were that boy! You were that rapscallion of a boy who lost my handkerchief!"

"You wiped the sweat from your face and your… neck with it." It suddenly dawns on her, "You didn't lose it, did you?"

"No. I did not. I kept it. And I've carried it with me, next to my heart, ever since."

"Well, well, well, you are a romantic young man, aren't you, Maestro Rossini? Quite the gallant! I'm touched. You can see I'm quite touched, can't you, Domenico?

"Yes, very touched, my dearest."

She turns back to Gioacchino, "Charming, maestro," she takes his hand again, "or may I call you, Gioacchino?"

"I would be honoured, Isabella."

"Till we meet again, Gioacchino."

She starts to process off stage then stops, and returns. She hands the handkerchief to Gioacchino. "Keep it – as a memento of me. Come Domenico!" and she does a full prima donna turn, and exits the stage.

Domenico takes a snuff-box out of his jacket, opens it, takes a large pinch between finger and thumb, sticks the finger and thumb into one nostril, then the other, spilling some of the snuff liberally down his waistcoat, and sniffing vociferously. "Why don't you come to my apartment, top floor, 210 Via Toledo, in, say, two hours from now, and we can discuss a few things, including a possible working relationship, yes? I assure you it will be greatly to your advantage."

"210 Via Toledo?" echoes Gioacchino.

"It is a little palazzo that I own. Five levels. Any local will know where it is and will direct you – for a fee of course – this is Naples."

"I will be there, Impresario."

Domenico bows to Gioacchino with a sweep of the arm. Gioacchino responds with an even lower, more florid bow.

Domenico beckons to his ever-present secretary who is hovering behind him, to attend him, and as soon as he is at Domenico's side, Domenico starts dictating, and Nicolo, the secretary, starts writing, expertly juggling quill, pot, and paper on his satchel, as is his way.

"A note to self… 'Elizabetta', Queen of England," he declaims, "a new opera to be composed by Signor Gioacchino Rossini, for a sum and on terms yet to be agreed, title role of Elizabetta to be played by Signorina Isabella Colbran, soprano, supported by Manuel Garcia, tenore, Andrea Nozzari, tenore…" and he strides off stage, with Nicolo running and scribbling behind him.

THIRTY

Italy

Barbaja's apartment 210 Via Toledo, Naples

Gioacchino is lounging on a chaise longue near the window. Secretary Nicolo is sitting cross-legged on the floor, inkpot on floor, paper on satchel, and quill in hand, furiously scribbling. Domenico Barbaja is pacing the length and breadth of the enormous room in his ground floor apartment in his palazzo, hands behind his back, dictating terms.

"Signor Gioacchino Rossini will commit to writing two new operas a year, every year, for five years, choice of such operas made by Signor Rossini, but subject to my approval of course, to be staged at the royal theatres under my management – Teatro San Carlo, or Teatro Fiorentini, or Teatro Fondo."

Nicolo races and scratches, trying to keep up with his master.

"Signor Rossini will also act as Musical Director of all my theatres and as such will oversee any other operas that Signor Barbaja may wish to produce…"

Nicolo whimpers, under stress, and scratches away.

119

Barbaja ignores the whimpers, in fact, he seems to speed up in his delivery, "… and will assume some administrative and managerial duties for the theatres…"

"What about your kitchen?" says Gioacchino, "I am a celebrated cook. Surely you'd want me to run your kitchen too?"

Nicolo looks up at Barbaja. but Barbaja ignores the interruption, in fact, does not seem to have even heard it. "In return," he announces, with great pomp and gravity, "he will receive the sum of 12,000 francs – which is 3,600 ducats – per year, a percentage of the gambling receipts from the said royal theatres, amounting to at least another 1,000 ducats." He stops and looks directly at Gioacchino, awaiting an astonished but sufficiently grateful response.

He gets no such response. Gioacchino knows only too well that he is being offered a handsome return, a guarantee of employment for years to come, an assured venue for all his operas – a composer's dream – but he is canny enough to say nothing at this point. Which is a very difficult thing for an Italian to do.

It works.

Domenico pats his breast pocket, searching for his snuff-box, does not find it there, screws up his face in annoyance, then looks back at Gioacchino and beams at him. It is a great piece of acting skill and control. "Plus," he announces grandly, "the use of the third-floor apartment in this palazzo, without cost, with free full board, providing easy access to and from the royal Teatro San Carlo."

He continues to beam at Gioacchino.

Gioacchino cannot believe his good fortune. It is a daunting contract – two operas per year, every year, plus Musical Director.

It would be too much for any composer. But, Gioacchino knows, Gioacchino Rossini is not any composer. And the returns!

"And the casts of the operas?" he asks.

"Your choice and my choice," responds Domenico.

"Including Signorina Colbran?"

"Especially Signorina Colbran!"

Gioacchino feels his groin stir just at the thought of it. He stands, picks up his hat, dons it, and bows. "I thank you, Signor Impresario Domenico Barbaja, and I promise I will think about your suggestions, most seriously, and will respond post-haste."

As soon as Gioacchino has left, Nicolo coughs politely to attract Domenico's attention. Domenico looks at him and nods.

"It is a very generous contract, Impresario."

"You think so."

"You have never offered such terms to any other composer."

"No, I have not – but I am also demanding an impossibility in return. No composer can deliver what I ask. So, he will fail."

"You want him to fail?"

"I want him to try. I expect him to deliver for the first couple of years, then inevitably founder and want out. And that suits me. I get four or five new operas, written by a musical genius. I reap the fame, the crowds that will flock to my theatres, the money they will spend for opera tickets and at my roulette tables, the undying gratitude of my singers – and then, Gioacchino Rossini will blow up, within two years, three at the most, I would hazard. Leaving me in sole charge of the battlefield and all its spoils. I predict this – and you can write that down on your little bits of paper as well, my friend."

THIRTY-ONE

Italy

The market in the teeming streets of Naples

Isabella is striding purposefully but regally, as she does always, everywhere, through a teeming Neapolitan market. She is accompanied by Gabriella, but also closely pursued by Maestro. The streets are thronged with shouting and yelling, buying and selling, arguing and bargaining Neapolitans, while carriages of the rich career along, double-file in the single lanes, as is the way of Naples.

Maestro is speaking to Isabella in a breathless torrent, on the run, and Isabella is deliberately not listening to him, not stopping, not pausing, not acknowledging that he is actually there. "I don't know how you mistook me, signora…" he dodges around a woman carrying a basket of fruit "… I was talking about Gioacchino, surely you know that! Not me. Good heavens, not me, I assure you, signora … couldn't be silly little me – what an absurd idea! Me! – I mean, I'm twice your age, right? Crazy idea!" and he laughs loudly to show her how crazy the idea is.

Isabella stops at a street stall which is selling steaming, hanging, cooked spaghetti. She buys some, raises it high above her head and lowers it into her mouth, eating as she lowers her hand.

"... it's just that I wanted to tell you how much Gioacchino admires you," wheedles Maestro, "and then I saw you – and it was more than any red-blooded man could stand! I mean, do you know what effect you have on men, signora? Do you? It was all your doing really – you can't seriously blame a poor old man like me, now can you?"

And Isabella turns abruptly, with Gabriella close behind, into a milliner's boutique, and Gabriella, looking Maestro in the eye with obvious satisfaction, pulls the door closed behind them, shutting it in his face.

Maestro continues talking to the closed door. "I've seen much bigger tits than yours, Isabella, I can assure you." He cups his hands to show himself just how large the ones he's seen were. "Enormous, whale tits that you could stick in your ears and shut out all sound – even your singing!" and he circles his hands around to insert the tits into his ears, and laughs. "And, as for your arse ..."

THIRTY-TWO

Italy

Backstage at Teatro San Carlo. Naples

There are four dishes set out in a line on a large table, backstage at Teatro San Carlo. Each dish has olive oil in it – a different oil in each dish so that each has a distinctive shade of colour: one more gold, one more green, one dark green-gold, one translucent. There is a platter of Italian bread, broken into mouth-sized pieces, next to the dishes. Isabella is standing close to the table. She is blindfolded. Gioacchino is standing behind her, holding her by the shoulders.

Domenico Barbaja watches, arms folded, unsmiling.

"One of the oils in front of you, Isabella," says Gioacchino, "is a first pressing, virgin oil, from the monastery of San Croce. It is like nectar, an ambrosia from the lips of the gods themselves. Find it. Dip some bread in each oil in turn and taste."

Isabella giggles and shuffles closer to the table.

"But ..." he laughs into her ear, "just so that it's not too easy, the other oils are also first pressings – but not San Croce!"

"Ooh! You nasty man you! Quick, some bread, I can't wait!"

And Gioacchino places a piece of bread in her hand and, with Gioacchino's help, she feels her way carefully with her other hand to the dishes. She dips the bread in one and tastes it.

"Mmmm!" is all she says, and she continues in similar vein until she has tasted all four. She whips off the blindfold, and cries in triumph, "This one – the first one! Yes?"

"I'm not telling."

"But you must!" she cries. "You can't be that cruel! I'm right, aren't I? I know I am, admit it!"

"I am saying nothing until Domenico here has tasted. I mean, Domenico is the inventor of the famous secret recipe for 'Barbajata', is he not? He's a connoisseur! An expert! We must get his opinion first. Yes, Domenico?"

"What is this 'Barbajata'?" asks Isabella, and she turns to look at Domenico.

Domenico opens his mouth but Gioacchino gets in first, "You don't know? I am amazed! Well, our dear Domenico here started off life as a waiter, and one day discovered the secret of mixing whipped cream with coffee and chocolate…"

"Ooh! Sounds divine! I want some, Domenico!" cries Isabella.

"… and made his fortune in the north, in Tuscana, Milano, Torino… am I right, Domenico?"

"You are always right, Gioacchino. So, I will go along with your little game," and he suddenly has a snuff-box in his hand – no one knows where it has come from – he takes a huge pinch, sticks his fingers in his nostrils and snorts loudly.

Gioacchino's eyes glint, "Then let's make it a real game. Find the San Croce oil, Domenico, and I will sign your contract to become musical director of your two opera houses and write your ten operas. Get it wrong – and you give me the recipe for the 'Barbajata'. Agreed?"

"Ooh!" cries Isabella. "Go on, Domenico, go on!"

"Agreed," says Domenico – with just a hint of gritted teeth.

Isabella hands Domenico the blindfold.

"There is one other condition," says Gioacchino.

"And what is that?" says Domenico, with more than just a hint this time.

"We add Isabella to the forfeit."

"Ooh!" breathes Isabella.

"What?" says Domenico.

"You heard me plain enough, I think, Domenico. Isabella?"

Isabella is beside herself with excitement, "It seems to me that I have nothing to lose – I win either way."

"Good, then we …"

"… but I also have a condition," continues Isabella.

"What?" says Gioacchino.

"What?" says Domenico.

"I always inspect my prosciutto carefully before I buy. No two hams are alike." She giggles. "Old hams taste of the earth – musty and strong. Young hams have the scent of fresh-cut hay. I will not simply accept either of you. Whoever wins has to woo me and court me – send me flowers, presents, billets-doux – and in the end, I might, just might, entertain him. Is that agreed?"

"Agreed," says Gioacchino immediately.

Domenico is starting to wonder if he has been set up, if there has been collusion here. After all, Isabella is already his, but he shrugs and mutters, "Agreed."

"Then let the games begin!" cries Isabella and she ties the blindfold over Domenico's eyes, stands behind him then places him in front of the dishes at the table.

Gioacchino quickly removes the first dish and replaces it with another dish from the sideboard.

Isabella's eyes flash and widen.

Gioacchino passes a piece of bread to Domenico. Domenico dips the bread into each dish in turn and tastes it. He then accepts another piece of bread, tries the second, then the third dish. He hesitates, confused, then feels for dish one again and re-tries it. He takes off his blindfold and shakes his head.

"Perhaps … this one …" he indicates the first dish, "or this …" he indicates the third dish, "I am not sure."

Isabella is triumphant. "It was the first. I was right!"

Gioacchino nods.

"In which case, Gioacchino, you win," says Domenico and he holds out his hand towards him.

"No," says Gioacchino, "we both win. I cheated, Domenico, and I do not wish to win by cheating – not unless I have to. I will sign your contract, on the original terms you offered – two new operas a year for five years, Musical Director, and so on and so on – including the terms of remuneration – and am happy to do so. As for Isabella, I have one request – not a condition, a request."

"And that is?" says Domenico.

"That Isabella is my prima donna in all ten operas."

"I would have expected nothing less," says Domenico. "Isabella? Your answer?"

"Elisabetta, if you please, Domenico," she says. "So, we all win, yes, gentlemen?"

THIRTY-THREE

Italy

Barbaja's apartment in palazzo
210 Via Toledo. Naples

Isabella is standing at the window of Domenico's ground floor apartment in the palazzo, 210 Via Toledo, Naples. Domenico owns the apartment, in fact, he owns all five floors of apartments in the palazzo. The view is of the busy, vibrant street.

"They say, 'See Naples and die", don't they, Domenico?" says Isabella, "but they should really be saying, 'Stand at the window in Domenico Barbaja's apartment in his beautiful palazzo on 210 Via Toledo and look out over the thoroughfare and sea beyond, and die', shouldn't they, Domenico?" and she laughs at her own witticism. "I love it every time I stand here."

"Or, perhaps more correctly," says Domenico, "it should be 'See Signorina Isabella Colbran standing at the window in Domenico Barbaja's apartment in his beautiful palazzo on 2102 Via Toledo…'"

Isabella laughs again at his cleverness, then asks, "Why didn't you tell me about this secret barbajata of yours?"

"No secret, my dear! The barbajata is famous in the north – in Milan, in Florence, throughout Tuscany, Venice, Rome…"

"But not in Naples. Why does it bear your name."

"Because I invented it."

"When you were a waiter…?"

"When I was a waiter."

"Is that why you didn't tell me about it? Are you ashamed that you were once a waiter, Domenico?"

"No! I am not! I am proud of being a waiter – because I was the best – charming, attentive, handsome, a favourite of the ladies…"

"Were you indeed!"

"… and inventive. I have a brain, my darling, and I have ideas…'

"Oh, I know," she says with a sigh, "and I also know what those ideas usually lead to…"

"I'm having one right now!" he says, and he takes his snuff-box from his jacket pocket, opens it, taps snuff onto the back of his hand and sniffs it vigorously.

"You are!"

"Yes!" He stuffs the box back into his jacket pocket, rips off his jacket without taking his eyes off hers, throws it to one side, and closes in on her so that their faces are almost touching.

"What if I…" and he stops.

There is a pause. Isabella waits, increasingly excited, but he doesn't speak.

"What if you what?" she squeals.

"What if I were to make you a Barbajata right now?"

"A Barbajata! Right now?" she breathes.

"With a thick layer of chocolate on the bottom…" his eyes flick down her body then back up to her face, "then a layer of coffee, silken, milk coffee, freshly ground…"

"…silken, milk coffee, freshly ground…" she breathes.

"… and smother it with cream, cream whipped by hand, my hand, covering the coffee beneath, and the hidden chocolate below…" he looks down and then up again, more slowly this time, "… deep down below…"

"Do it!" she gasps. "Do it now!"

Isabella is lying on the huge bed in Domenico's apartment in the palazzo, 210 Via Toledo. Nude, her hands clasped behind her head, satisfied, even happy.

She can hear Domenico in the kitchen, stirring a spoon in a glass, then in another glass, a faint plop, another faint plop, and he comes into the bedroom, nude, a glass in each hand, a glass dark at the bottom, bronze-coloured above, and topped with white whipped cream. He holds out a glass to her. She accepts it. He sits on the bed. They touch glasses, breathe 'Salute', and sip.

"Mmmm," murmurs Isabella, and she sips again.

THIRTY-FOUR

Italy

Teatro San Carlo. Naples

And Barbaja is true to his word.
He decides he will produce an opera, in 'Elizabetta', the like of which that the world has never seen – to match the magnificence of Teatro San Carlo, one of the oldest opera houses in Europe, with all its blue and gold, its one thousand four hundred seats, its one hundred and eighty four boxes, with their blue upholstery and gold ornamentation, their carved sconces and plate mirrors reflecting the glittering candlelight, all added to the unparalleled beauty, stature, and voice of Isabella Colbran in the lead role, the glittering support cast of singers and dancers, he, Domenico Barbaja, will add authenticity. He sends secretary Nicolo, with servants and pockets of money, to London, to view, talk about, buy samples of, buy portraits of Elizabethan furniture, costumes, fashions, colours, from the English aristocracy who will do anything for money and prestige, from museums, private collections…

Isabella sends her maid, Gabriella, to the third-floor apartment in the palazzo at 210 Via Toledo, and to slip a message to Gioacchino under his door, suggesting that he and she meet at her rooms.

Gioacchino rushes round there. She ushers him in and points at a chair, facing a table, without a word said. He sits.

She sits opposite him and tosses a note down onto the table between them. Gioacchino glances at it and at the hand-writing on the front, and takes a note from his jacket pocket, and tosses it onto the table next to hers. The hand-writing is the same.

Gioacchino picks up her note and reads the salutation on the front aloud, "My Dere Isabella," pronouncing it exactly as it is spelt. He makes no comment, opens the note, and continues to read out loud, pronouncing each word as it is spelt, "Dere Isabella, I ave Mutch… with a capital… pleaser in invaiting you and my Dere fiend Goccinno…"

"I know! I know!" cries, Isabella, "it's beautiful!… my dere fiend…it's so wonderfully bad… that it's beautiful!"

"… you and my Dere fiend Goccinno to a Latte… with a capital… super at my palaazo this Ivening… with a capital… by coglioni!… well, he's got 'balls' spelled correctly anyway… strange that, is it not… and ending with a flourish… You devotted Domenico."

There is a long pause, then both burst out laughing and laughing and laughing. "A true work of art!" announces Gioacchino when he has recovered enough. He picks up his note from the table and reads the salutation on the front aloud, as spelt, "My Dere Goccinno…" but he cannot continue… and they both burst out laughing again.

"Does he know?" wonders Isabella.

"Almost certainly, yes."

"Does he care?"

"Almost certainly, no."

"He can't – otherwise he wouldn't write the notes to us."

"Suddenly, it is very clear why secretary Nicolo follows our dere fiend, Domenico, everywhere, like a bad smell," says Gioacchino.

"And dere fiend, Nicolo, is, of course, in England at the moment," adds Isabella, "which is why Domenico has written the notes himself..."

"Domenico clearly never attended school. He is illiterate... he cannot spell... capital letters are complete mystery..."

"... and yet, he is probably the richest man in Naples," says Isabella. "He has a genius for making money. He manages three opera houses, he owns gambling halls with countless roulette tables, a villa on the island of Ischia, a palazzo in Possilipo, complete with private theatre that seats three hundred people, a palazzo at 210 Via Toledo..."

"... and he dines with princes and kings!" crows Gioacchino. "They obviously regard him as their dere fiend!"

"... which makes him all the more impressive, does it not?" says Isabella.

"Impressive, yes! Surprising, yes! Amazing, yes!" answers Gioacchino, "but also, a worry, no? What other secrets does he have? Who knows the real Domenico Barbaja?"

"Perhaps nobody..." whispers Isabella.

"Oh, I think I know of someone who knows," says Gioacchino.

"Who?" laughs Isabella.

"His wife," says Gioacchino.

"His wife?" gasps Isabella.

"Signora Rosa Gerbini, I think her name is. He left her in Milan with the two children when he came south to Naples."

"Two children!"

"Yes. Haven't met them, but I think it's a boy and a girl."

Isabella's face is white. She holds her breath, sucks in air, then holds her breath again.

Perhaps she has eaten too much, thinks Gioacchino, or perhaps she has been laughing too much.

"Coglioni!" spits Isabella.

Gioacchino smiles. An excellent day!

Gioacchino goes to the supper at Domenico's apartment that evening. It is just the two of them. Isabella is indisposed, for some reason. They scoff pasta, drink wine, and sing vociferously until the early hours of the following morning.

THIRTY-FIVE

Italy

Teatro San Carlo. Naples

Isabella is singing Elizabetta's 'Bell' alme generose' aria to Leicester and Matilde from Gioacchino Rossini's 'Elisabetta, regina d'Inghilterra'. And Isabella is the quintessential queen – stunningly beautiful, commanding, with flashing eyes and minimal gesture, richly attired, radiating majesty, and all delivered in her rich, powerful voice, and causing the audience to leap to its feet with "Bravas" and "Vivas", while she is still singing, as is the Italian way, constantly interrupting her but not affecting her, in fact, enthusing her. It is a musical bedlam that sends Gioacchino, in the orchestra pit, and Domenico, in his box, into raptures.

"Brava! Brava!" calls Domenico repeatedly and thumps the balustrade with such force that those below fear for their safety. And, on one occasion, when a partisan Neapolitan voiced his disapproval of the Spanish soprano because she was not a Neapolitan, Domenico orders his stewards to forcibly remove the deluded culprit with thundered promises emanating from the box that he would never be allowed back into the theatre.

When she finishes her seemingly unending bows, Isabella rushes to her dressing-room. She is closely followed by Gioacchino. The cries of the audience are still ringing in their ears. Gioacchino closes the door behind him and locks it. Isabella spins around to look at him.

"Brava! Brava! Brava!" he breathes. "Words cannot describe your performance tonight, Isabella, or what I feel for you. I have never been happier in my life."

"Nor I, Gioacchino."

Gioacchino moves towards her, like a cat stalking its prey. Isabella's eyes widen. She backs away, not once taking her eyes off him, inviting him, daring him. She reaches the dressing table and stops. Gioacchino steps forward and bows and salutes her in full Elizabethan flourish. "Your majesty! Would you be so kind as to allow your humble servant to disrobe you?"

Isabella is so excited she has difficulty speaking, "Disrobe me, sir?"

"If your majesty wishes."

"Oh, her majesty does wish, sir."

And very slowly and very deliberately, Gioacchino reaches up and removes the crown and jewels from her hair, whispering as he does, "Of all its wreathed pearls her hair he frees …" He undoes the hooks in her bodice, easing it off her shoulders, until it falls about her, like a mermaid in seaweed, whispering as he does so, "… unclasps her warmed jewels, one by one, loosens her fragrant bodice, by degrees her rich attire creeps rustling to her knees …"

Gioacchino stretches up and she anticipates his goal and bends forward to meet him. He kisses her on the lips, just touching, a caress of a kiss.

She lifts her hands to his head and slowly pulls his head forward between her breasts.

There is a rattle of the door handle, then loud knocking at the door.

"Isabella! Bella!" Domenico's voice. "Let us in!"

Which Gioacchino and Isabella completely ignore, as if he were not there, as if he hasn't spoken at all, as they go about the sacred business of love.

All of Naples is ecstatic," writes the celebrated writer and critic, Stendhal, who was in the stalls that first night, "As Queen Elizabeth, Colbran used no gestures, did nothing melodramatic, never descended to what are vulgarly called 'tragedy-queen poses'. In all the huge arena of the San Carlo, there can scarcely have been a man who had not, at that moment, thought death an insignificant price to pay for a glance from so beautiful a Queen."

Lavish words of praise indeed.

And Isabella and Gioacchino spend many excellent days and nights together from this day on. They are inseparable. They are either in bed in her rooms or in bed in his apartment in the palazzo at 210 Via Toledo. Much to the annoyance and mounting fury of Domenico Barbaja. Much to the annoyance and mounting frustration of Maestro.

Because there is work to be done. 'Otello' has been promised, under contract, but hasn't even been started.

But Fortune takes a hand in the affairs of men and women.

On the night of 13 February, 1816, during a rehearsal for a ball, a fire breaks out in the storage room for lights and torches in Teatro San Carlo, spreads quickly to the stage and theatre proper and, within moments, the whole is engulfed in flames. The royal family rushes out of their palace to watch, but are helpless to do anything. The fire brigade had recently been disbanded in an effort to save money.

Domenico rushes to the theatre while the fires burn and ensures his gold stored in the vault is rescued, which it is, under his direction.

Domenico makes a personal commitment to the king to rebuild the theatre within 300 days, and King Ferdinand appoints him to manage the reconstruction. Domenico starts work immediately.

THIRTY-SIX

Italy

Gioacchino's apartment in palazzo
210 Via Toledo. Naples

'Otello' is late. More than late. Gioacchino has not even started writing. Gioacchino tells Domenico that he has ideas for the opera but there are good reasons why he has not started – San Carlo has burned to the ground so there is no theatre to house the opera in. Teatro del Fiorentini, says Domenico. Too small, says Gioacchino. Teatro del Fondo, says Domenico. It is the theatre where comic opera is performed, says Gioacchino, and Otello is not comic. It is an opera seria. At least start, says Domenico. I do not write that way, says Gioacchino, I write in a flood, in a passion, not in episodes.

Domenico screams and rants and threatens and issues an edict that Isabella is not to stay in his apartment at 210 Via Toledo. So Gioacchino sleeps with Isabella in Isabella's rooms.

Domenico tries bribery. He hires two Sicilian chefs and offers to cook Gioacchino his favourite 'maccheroni alla napoletana'. Gioacchino accepts the invitation, eats his favourite meal, thanks the chefs and his host, and returns to his life of sloth and sex.

Maestro is beside himself. He climbs the outside stairs to Gioacchino's third floor apartment and raps on the door at all hours of the day and night, a fact observed and noted by Domenico, to either find Gioacchino in bed with Isabella, day or night, or simply absent. "And we know where!" Maestro says to himself.

Part of the problem with 'Otello', which was chosen by both Gioacchino and Barbaja, is the librettist. 'Otello', the opera, was to be based on 'Othello', the play by Englishman, William Shakespeare. However, Barbaja, unilaterally chooses Francesco Maria Berio as the librettist for the opera. There are a number of reasons for this choice. First and foremost, Berio is the Marquis of Salsa, an aristocrat and strong supporter of and favourite of King Ferdinand of Naples, Barbaja's friend and backer. Second, Berio di Salsa is a personal friend of Barbaja himself. Berio owns a Palazzo on Via Toledo, very close to Barbaja's palazzo in Via Toledo, and just as splendid, if not more splendid than Barbaja's, with an imposing entranceway, a ballroom, a private theatre with a sculpture by the famous Venetian artist, Antonio Canova, a shopping arcade on street level with arches designed by prominent architect, Luigi Vanvitelli, and a marble fountain with a sculpted deer's head. Where he entertained some of the artists and aristocrats of nineteenth century Europe. Unfortunately, Berio di Salsa is a fop and literary dilettante, and the resulting Libretto reflects this. Stendhal describes Berio as "the unmentionable literary hack."

Domenico Barbaja's decision to appoint Berio di Salsa was clearly an act of political genius, and equally as clearly, an artistic disaster.

Added to this is Gioacchino's prevarication.

Domenico's requests, pleadings, bribes, rants, threats, and edicts, have all failed. And when Domenico is forced to reimburse his opera box-owners' subscriptions, and with only a few weeks to go before the first scheduled rehearsal, Domenico's patience snaps.

Gioacchino wakes one morning and rings his servant's bell. No one answers. Gioacchino is forced to get up from bed and investigate. The apartment, he discovers, is empty. The front door is locked. And it has been bolted from the outside. Domenico has locked the celebrated composer, Gioacchino Rossini, inside his apartment.

Gioacchino goes out onto his balcony and stares out and down. The balcony is seven to eight metres from the ground – too high and certainly too dangerous to climb down. Gioacchino goes back to bed. An hour later, he gets up and goes back out onto his balcony. He calls out for someone, anyone, to help him. All passers-by ignore him, of course. This is Naples.

Gioacchino leans out, faces upwards, and calls out to Barbaja. "Domenico!"

For some reason, Domenico does not respond. Gioacchino calls out again and keeps calling out until many minutes later, a head appears on Domenico's balcony two levels below, and looks up at him. It is Domenico.

"Good morning!' calls Domenico. "What a beautiful day, isn't it? Did you want something, my friend?"

"Want something? Want something? I want out!" screams Gioacchino.

"Do you, my friend?"

"I am clearly not your friend, my friend – more like my fiend, my dere fiend!"

"Now you are talking gibberish, my friend," he laughs. "Now, how can I help?"

"You are clearly the one who has locked me in, so you can let me out!"

"Certainly! I will let you out the minute you deliver to me a completed score of the opera, 'Otello'."

"The completed score? Are you mad? I haven't even started the score – that could take days, weeks…"

"Oh, I know! I know!"

"I could starve…"

"No, no, no," laughs Domenico. "I will get my Sicilian chefs to make you your favourite dish – 'maccheroni alla napolitana' – every day, every week, till you have finished. You won't starve, my friend. You might get a little larger, but you won't starve."

"Stop calling me your friend, you fiend. You are clearly not my friend."

"Oh, but I clearly am – free food, free lodging – that's what a true friend does, my friend."

Gioacchino starts circling his balcony. He goes inside his apartment, comes out again almost immediately, and circles the balcony again. He stops and stares over. Domenico is not there!

"Domenico!" he calls.

Domenico's head reappears below. "I thought you'd gone for a lie-down or something. Yes, how can I help?"

"I will… I will get the Overture to 'Otello' delivered to you this evening."

"The Overture! This evening?" says Domenico. "Oh, that is very good."

"And you will set me free as soon as you receive it."

"No, my friend, I will not. I will gladly accept the Overture this evening. I will invite guests around, and we will celebrate your name when I receive it, but you will only be set free when I have the complete score."

"Aagh!" cries Gioacchino and he disappears inside.

"Va bene, my friend!" cries Domenico and he disappears inside.

An hour later there is a knock on the door of the third-floor apartment at 210 Via Toledo.

Gioacchino rushes to the door. "Yes? Who is it?" he cries.

"It's me, Maestro."

"Thank goodness for that!"

Maestro waits. Nothing happens,

"Well, let me in!"

"I can't!"

"Why not? Is she here?"

"Who is 'she'?"

"Isabella of course!"

"No, she's not here – I'm the only one here."

"Then let me in!"

"I can't open the door. It's locked!"

Maestro looks at the door, sees it is bolted from the outside, unbolts it and pushes the door. It does not move.

"The door itself is locked!" cries Gioacchino.

"The door itself? Who would lock your door?"

"The fiend!"

"Now this is starting to become very silly, Gioacchino. What fiend are you talking about?"

"Domenico Barbaja!"

"Domenico locked you in? Why?"

"Because he's a fiend, a fiend from Hell!"

"But even a fiend from Hell usually has a reason for being a fiend, Gioacchino. What did you do?"

"It's more what I didn't do," says Gioacchino, suddenly speaking very quietly indeed.

"What do you mean? Speak up, I can't hear you through the door."

"Otello!" says Gioacchino, screaming again. "We didn't write his damned Otello for him!"

There is a long pause outside the door, while Maestro digests this information.

"No, we didn't," says Maestro eventually.

"And he's not letting me out of this place till we've written the score – the whole score, mind you!"

"Isn't he? Well, well, what a fiend! But my friend – and I'm sorry, but I have to say this – I think the fiend is right. We should have written the score of Otello weeks ago."

"You are on his side!"

"If you put it like that, then yes, I am on his side. But it's the truth."

"So, you'll be happy that I promised to finish the Overture by tonight!" says Gioacchino with more than a hint of sarcasm.

"Tonight?"

"Yes – well, this evening, actually."

"Then we'd better get started then, hadn't we?"

And so they hum and tap and sing and write hurrying strings, leading into a solo clarinet suggesting a mood of heart-rending pity, followed by an allegro that is downright vivacious…

"… too vivacious perhaps, says Gioacchino."

"Perhaps your reserve, my friend, can be put down to your ill-temper this morning – understandable ill-temper, I hasten to add, seeing as you probably haven't eaten yet – but I suggest that you reconsider and try to be your normal vivacious self."

At which Gioacchino laughs and agrees.

And so, two of the greatest composers the world has ever known, soldier on with the Overture to the opera, Otello, one on each side of a door. Gioacchino writes down the score for all parts onto paper because Maestro decides the score will need to be recognizable as Gioacchino's writing and penmanship, and because Maestro doesn't have any paper on his side of the door anyway.

Another hour later, Maestro has to scurry. He hears the fluted voice of Diva Isabella Colbran below as she gives her maid, Gabriella, her orders, then hurries up.

Maestro himself hurries up the stairs to the fourth level and ducks out of sight. He hears every word of the conversation below between Isabella and Gioacchino – an almost word-for-word reprise of his earlier exchange on the same subject with Gioacchino.

Isabella is appalled. She is outraged. Her talented, wonderful, thoughtful, loving little Gioacchi-Woacchi to be treated in such a rude, disrespectful manner! By such a fiend! She would beard the monster herself! In his den! Right now! Which she does. And gets absolutely nowhere.

Domenico laughs at her outrage, scorns her concern for her little Gioacchi-Woacchi – for he'd heard every word of their earlier exchange, he tells her, from his balcony below. He suggests she go home and practice her scales ready for the Desdemona role in Otello because the music was destined to meet the daylight very soon indeed.

Isabella disappears in a righteous huff.

In the early afternoon, Maestro and Gioacchino are interrupted again when two burly Sicilian chefs come out of Domenico's apartment below and climb the stairs.

Maestro quickly re-bolts the door and reclaims his sanctuary on the floor above.

One chef unlocks Gioacchino's door but holds onto it firmly

so that there is no possibility of Gioacchino getting past him, while the second chef is let through the doorway sufficient to place a large, steaming bowl of maccheroni alla Napoletana on the floor inside the apartment. He looks up at Gioacchino, smiles widely, wishes him a hearty "Buon appetito!", closes the door with a thud, locks it securely, and re-bolts it from the outside.

They disappear down the stairs.

Maestro returns to his post next to Gioacchino's door. The pasta is on the inside, of course, out of reach, and Maestro has had no food. The two decide to adjourn for a late lunch – Gioacchino inside, already tucking into his favourite pasta, and Maestro down the street at a caffè.

At a very respectable time for any Italian to be eating his evening meal, Maestro knocks on Domenico's door on the ground floor. Domenico answers the door himself. Maestro tells him that his friend, Gioacchino Rossini, in the apartment two floors above, passed him a copy of a completed Overture to the opera 'Otello' under the bottom of his door, and requested that he deliver it into the hands of one Domenico Barbaja who lives in the apartment on the ground floor of the palazzo.

"Do you know Signor Domenico Barbaja, signor?" asks Maestro, absolutely straight-faced.

"I do indeed, signor. I am Domenico Barbaja."

"Excellent," and he hands a bundle of manuscript papers to Domenico.

"Would you wait here a moment please?" says Domenico and he disappears inside.

Maestro waits, and hears a piano start up inside. The pianist plays the opening of the Overture, jumps to the clarinet solo, jumps again to the vivacious allegro – and is greeted with a series of 'Bravos' and then a shout of 'The Swan of Pesaro!' in Domenico's distinctive voice.

Domenico returns to the door and the waiting Maestro.

"Tell your master…"

"He is not my master, Signor," cuts in Maestro. "He is a friend, no more, no less."

"Then tell your… friend… that we find his offering this evening to be satisfactory, and that we look forward to seeing the rest with the opera in the near future."

After a week, Gioacchino is a raging bull, or a spoilt child, or a typical temperamental Northerner from Bologna, or a poor little Gioacchi-Woacchi, depending on who is speaking, of course. It's not the work, not the composing through a door, not the not being able to sink his head between the smothering breasts of his 'Bella, not the bullying tactics of his one-time friend, Domenico Barbaja, not even being imprisoned in his rooms. It's the food. The same food. Every day, every meal. He hates the sight now of his one-time favourite pasta, his maccheroni alla damned napoletana!

He has a tantrum when the chefs arrive and demands something different. They ignore him, wish him 'Buon Appetito!', and disappear. He throws it back at them the next time they arrive. They ignore him and the mess, wish him 'Buon Appetito!', and disappear.

The next morning, a very unhappy Gioacchino comes to the door and gasps to the faithfully waiting Maestro, "My friend, I have had such a dream! I was wrapping a slice of foie gras around a Dover sole and cooking it in foil with half a shallot and half a truffle. And then I ate it! Heaven does not have such a dish!"

"You can make one for me when you get out of gaol, my friend," says Maestro.

"And when I finished the sole… there, in front of me, appeared a dessert – a dessert for the angels – a glass with ladyfingers topped with strawberry *coulis* and sliced strawberries, then a mound of mascarpone cream, blackberries and raspberries, and finally, on top of that, a scoop of strawberry sorbet."

"You will make yourself mad with such dreams, my friend."

"And then I woke up before I could eat it!"

"You are already mad, my friend."

"Bring me something, Maestro – anything… anything except pasta… please!"

"Something that will fit under the bottom of the door perhaps?" says Maestro. And Maestro buys wafers, savoury and sweet, and slips them under the door. Which proves a very, very temporary solution for the ravenous Gioacchino.

Isabella comes to the rescue of her Gioacchi-Woacchi. She buys fruit – everything in season, and stands on the ground level and throws them up to Gioacchino's balcony. Except that very few successfully land on Gioacchino's balcony. In fact, only one does, and that is a fairly ripe peach which bruises badly when Gioacchino succeeds in catching it. The rest of the fruit do not reach his balcony. They wilfully return to the ground and splatter or bounce and roll away or stick to a wall, or land on the balcony of apartment number two on the second level, where they are gratefully received and kept, if in good condition and if the occupants like that particular fruit, or are thrown back down because they are not or do not.

But Isabella's valiant efforts are abruptly ended when Domenico comes out and demands she cease fouling his palazzo. Isabella waves to a disconsolate Gioacchino on the third floor, and retires, defeated.

Maestro has been watching Isabella's efforts from a distance. He has made no attempt to help, as he has been a persona non grata to Isabella ever since her outrageous performance in her bathtub that day. He waits till she is gone then climbs the stairs to Gioacchino's landing, and knocks.

Signor Disgruntlement comes to the door. "Yes?" he says.

"My friend, it is obvious why your 'dere fiend' is doing what he is doing."

"And what is that?"

"To get you to a point where you realise that the only solution is to finish the score for 'Otello' as soon as possible. He is very clever. He is kind, he is feeding you, but he is not going to change the diet from your favourite dish one iota, so that you are even more motivated to get out – and the only way you can do that, is to complete the opera. I am very impressed."

And so, despite petulances and sulks, the opera of three tenors, and the magnificent role of Othello's Desdemona (written for Diva Signorina Isabella Colbran, of course) was born. The combination of three, high, male, tenor voices are debated and argued over for some days by Maestro and Gioacchino, but in the end, would prove immensely effective, especially during Othello's and Roderigo's Act Two confrontation, when top 'Cs' are exploding all over the place. As for Isabella's Desdemona role, the music ensures that she commands the final Act, especially when she is to be interrupted by a gondolier singing lines from Dante's Inferno. This brilliant piece of writing is followed by the haunting 'Willow Song" with minor-key, chromatic folk harmonies and ethereal orchestration for harp, strings and wind, that perfectly demonstrates the sheer talent and skill of the two composing geniuses.

But even these achievements are not without further evidence of Gioacchino's temper and temperament, when, one day shortly before they finish, he refuses to get out of bed, and only comes to the door because of Maestro's persistence, to pass a bundle of music – manuscripts – under the door to Maestro and demand that he deliver them to the fiend as that day's effort. After a single glance, Maestro recognises the sheets as the same music that was delivered the day before. He confronts the retreating Gioacchino with this fact.

"He won't know," calls out Gioacchino. "The fiend can't read music. He won't know!"

As it turns out, Gioacchino is correct. But only for half a day. Barbaja suspects something because of Maestro's manner when he delivers the sheets. Barbaja may not be able to read music, but he has an extraordinary talent for reading people. And he detects unease. An indefinable unease. He gets a colleague to check the music and, of course, is told of the ruse. Surprisingly, Domenico does not get angry. He sends the music back with a simple note, slipped under Gioacchino's door, saying, "A good try! Now try again."

And the opera is finished.

The first thing that Gioacchino does in the second that the final act of 'Otello' is delivered, checked against possible deceit, the door unlocked when it is passed as fit, and he is released from prison, is to scoot to the local pasticceria and wolf down four Cannoli Siciliano consisting of tube-shaped shells of fried pastry dough, filled with a sweet, creamy ricotta filling, then he consumed a plate of warm, Sicilian delicacies made from shortcrust pastry, filled with lemon custard, chocolate and cherries, called Pasticciotti.

At this point he confesses he is feeling a little sick, and would wait an hour perhaps, before he tucks into the Pheasant Suprême, stuffed with butter, foie gras, and, of course, slices of truffle, that he had ordered the day before.

'Otello' debuts in December 1816 at Teatro del Fondo, Domenico's other opera house in Naples, only a few blocks away from Teatro San Carlo which is still under reconstruction, progressing remarkably well, but not yet complete. The main cast is Andrea Nozzari, tenor, as Otello, and his rival, Giovanni David, as Roderigo. Desdemona is, of course, Signorina Isabella Colbran.

And the response from the Neapolitans at the première is mixed – 'Loved the music, hated the libretto' – was the general consensus.

Then in March 2107, 'Otello' debuts at the newly re-built Teatro San Carlo, where both the opera and the theatre are declared a resounding success.

The new San Carlo, rebuilt in three hundred days, is even more grand, more lavish, and more impressive than the old. It seats in excess of two thousand, five hundred spectators, the stalls alone hold over six hundred and seventy people in nineteen rows of sofas and seats, allowing for standing room for one hundred and fifty people at the back.

'The Auditorium,' says famous critic, Stendhal, 'is gold and silver, and the boxes are as blue as the sky. The balustrades of the boxes are ornamented with reliefs, that project magnificently… the boxes have no curtains and are rather spacious. I see five or six people in all the first rows. There is a superb chandelier, glittering with light, which makes all the gold and silver ornaments sparkle throughout…'

The massive, crystal chandelier, that Stendhal describes, has three rows of oil lamps, one hundred and eight in total, and when added to the two thousand wax candles, they create 'a triumph of lights'.

There are six dining and function rooms, built beneath the main foyer, which, to prevent any risk of fire, is fireproofed and encased in metal.

The total cost is massive – 241,000 ducats – part of which is borne by Barbaja himself.

And both Domenico Barbaja, for his role in the re-building of the new, stunningly beautiful theatre of Teatro San Carlo, and Gioacchino Rossini, for his perceived genius in composing such a stirring masterpiece as 'Otello', become the toast of Naples.

THIRTY-SEVEN

Italy

A caffè in Naples

Maestro is seated in his regular caffè in Via Toledo, close to Gioacchino's apartment. He sits alone, at a corner table. Away from the bright light and the other customers. He sips from a glass of white wine as he writes on sheets of manuscript paper.

Domenico Barbaja enters and, without asking permission, picks up a chair, carries it to Maestro's table, puts it down opposite Maestro, and sits on it.

Maestro stares at him but says nothing.

"In Piazza della Repubblica in Florence, there is a caffè called Caffè Giubbe Rosse," Domenico says, the instant he is seated, "and in it sits a man who is a writer. The caffè is a meeting place for artists – artists of all kinds – painters, sculptors, writers, and composers. Do you know it?"

"I may have seen it," responds Maestro.

Domenico takes his snuff-box from his jacket pocket and offers it to Maestro. Maestro declines. Reluctantly, Domenico puts the box back into his pocket without taking a pinch himself, such restraint, and continues as if there has been no interruption. "This Writer sits at the same table each day, all day. He drinks coffee, eats lunch, goes to the toilet, sometimes goes out front for a stretch and a very occasional conversation with a colleague or friend or who knows who, but, apart from those distractions, he simply works from the moment he arrives, till the moment he leaves. He writes on paper. Just like you."

"Why are you telling me this, Signor Barbaja?" asks Maestro.

"You remember my name. What is your name, pray?"

"Not important. People call me Maestro."

"Just Maestro?"

Maestro nods.

"Well Maestro, I don't swallow the mush you fed me that night you delivered the Overture of 'Otello'."

"What mush are you talking about?"

"That you are merely a friend of Gioacchino Rossini, who happened to be passing…"

"I did not say that."

"… perhaps I am exaggerating, just a little. Forgive me, but I think you are much more than you would have people believe. I have seen you often in my palazzo in Via Toledo in the company of my court composer…" He laughs at his jest, "I like that concept, don't you? My court composer… allow me my little conceit, my friend – I hope I may call you friend – may I?"

Maestro shrugs.

"Good. So, my friend, let me finish my story… every now and

then, someone comes in and sits at The Writer's table before the Writer gets there in the morning. The waiting staff look but say nothing. The composer arrives and is instantly agitated, like a chicken off his favourite perch. He paces, not angry, simply agitato. A waiter then quietly explains to the usurper that the musician has been sitting at that table each day, apart from sickness and for a morning on the death of his mother, for thirty years. The usurper always nods, understands how it is, and moves. The Writer sits and immediately starts work, laying out his paper and pen. He says nothing in thanks or acknowledgement – clearly focused on making up for the lost time."

"I repeat – why are you telling me this?" says Maestro.

"Because you are this man. You are in here in Naples, of course. You live in this world, but you are not part of this world. You live on your own, you have no family around you, just like my Writer, you come here each day – when you are not with our dear court composer... and you write. Strange, would you not agree?"

"How do you know this?"

"I have been observing you, and my spies – yes, I have spies – have been observing you. For many weeks now. But we are little the wiser for it. I still do not know who you are. Who are you, my friend? What are you?"

"Who are you? What are you, Impresario Barbaja?" says Maestro. "You are wealthy. You run theatres. You own gambling casinos. You are successful in everything you do..."

"I wouldn't say everything..."

"... you are feared. You are a passionate man, violent at times, I hear. People are very careful around you..."

"With good reason…"

"… and you are alone."

Domenico starts to say something but stops, leans back in his chair, and considers Maestro.

"That is a very astute observation, my friend, and perhaps a little dangerous. Which does not mean it is wrong, of course – I was not alone till your little friend came along."

"You are referring to Signor Rossini and Signorina Colbran, I presume."

"I am referring to your Gioacchino and my Isabella, who are fucking like rabbits…"

"… fucking like rabbits…"

"… when, until very recently, I was the only buck in the hutch, and doing all the fucking!" cries Domenico.

And, much to Domenico's astonishment and the astonishment of the caffè owner and all his clientèle, Maestro emits a long, wailing, baying laugh.

No one speaks. Everyone stares at Maestro. Maestro looks around at the open mouths and the open stares, and emits another long, wailing, baying laugh.

The owner starts to move forward. Domenico waves him away. He retreats. Everyone knows Domenico Barbaja. Domenico waits until Maestro is quiet and seemingly calm again – emitting only the occasional whimper of a laugh, and not a caterwauling.

Then surprisingly, Maestro leans forward and whispers, "My friend, you do not know what music that is to my ears."

"What music?"

"This may come as something of a surprise, but I am as opposed to the unnatural coupling of our two friends, as you understandably are. Isabella is a distraction to Gioacchino. She is a side-alley he should not be going down…" Maestro is getting more and more excited and speaking faster and faster as he goes on "… she is temporary, she is a transient affliction, she is all breasts and backside… and she is stopping my friend from doing what he was put on this earth to do – to write sublime music…" He stops and sucks in a big breath, "… and not to fuck like a rabbit."

There is a long pause as Domenico restrains the urge to laugh and takes in what he has just heard.

"… to write sublime music… with you, you mean?" he says quietly.

"What are you talking about, Signor?"

"Let's end the pretence here, my friend. I know that you write with him. I know that you and he composed 'Otello' together – one outside the door, one inside the door – that 'Otello' was a Rossini Maestro opera."

"You can't say that!"

"Oh, yes I can. As much as anyone could say it was a Rossini Berio di Salsa opera. No one could write that much music so quickly, in so short a time, of such quality – no one man could anyway. But two could. And that's exactly what happened, isn't it, Maestro? You collaborated. I'm right, aren't I?"

"I may… I may have helped a little here and there…

"Right."

"… because he was under such pressure from you – you imprisoned him…"

"Right."

"… he was starving and starting to go mad…"

"Enough! Enough! Maestro. I am not accusing you – or him – of anything. I am not blaming you – I understand, I understand. The question is, what are we going to do about it?"

"… going to do about what?"

"How I am going to get what I want… and how you are going to get what you want?"

THIRTY-EIGHT

Italy

Gioacchino's rooms 210 Via Toledo. Naples

Gioacchino and Maestro are working together feverishly by candle-light, writing on manuscript, on scraps of paper, as the rush of ideas is upon them. They hum snatches of melody from their new opera, La Cenerentola, they add harmony, they add accompaniments, singing the violins, the oboes, the brass, separately and together, of the opera that is to come. They sweat and swear, cursing it and themselves – and loving the joy and agony of it. Regularly, during the process, Maestro swigs from his ever-present flask of laudanum.

Maestro leans back in his chair and peers closely at Gioacchino. "You've been thinking with your balls, Gioacchino," he says.

"Have I?" says Gioacchino, and he scratches them.

"Yes! You're a great comic opera composer! This is your métier. This is your strength."

"Yours too."

"Yes! Mine too. That is precisely the point! We pull together, you and me. We are the best. But, unfortunately, she has seduced you. And she is destroying us."

"You mean Isabella."

"Of course I mean Isabella! You look at her face and you see her fanny, and in that instant your brain is mush. You write opera buffa brilliantly, Gioacchino. I write opera buffa brilliantly, Gioacchino. The Cenerentola characters are fun. They will make people laugh. Isabella doesn't make people laugh. She frightens them!"

Gioacchino scratches his balls again provocatively.

Maestro does not laugh.

Gioacchino looks at Maestro, square on. "I think you're being a little harsh there, my friend."

"Am I?" says Maestro, and he turns square on also, so that they look like bantams, but bantams too tired to fly, let alone tear. "Since we came to Naples you've written operas only for her – opera serie – where people die and die and die – I mean, Queen Elisabeth chops off some poor bastard's head, has a piss, paints her face, comes back on and chops off a cousin's head. Oh, bundle of laughs, isn't it?"

"You've written them with me."

"Of course I've written them with you – if I hadn't written them with you there would be no …" and Maestro stops, mouth open. He turns to a bottle of grappa, pours himself a large draught and downs it, all in one movement.

"Be no what?" says Gioacchino, quiet.

Maestro ignores the question. "Then there's Otello – you know what the critics are saying?"

"Be no what?" Louder.

Maestro rushes on, in a flurry of words, wanting to go back, wanting to erase, undo, "'The music's wonderful', they say – magnanimous of them, yes? '… but Rossini is crucifying Othello into an opera', they say! The story is butchered – a handkerchief turns into a love letter, and Othello himself, a black man, with a face as white as my mother's tits!"

"But that's the fault of the man who wrote the story – the librettist – not me!"

"Oh, I apologise! And whose name will people mention when they remember your opera?" He adopts a sycophantic voice, 'Otello? That wasn't written by Rossini! No, that was written by a librettist, Berio di Salsa!' My arse they will!"

"But it's had over thirty performances, all sold out – the audiences love it!"

"And there's your second problem, Gioacchino, my friend. It's bad enough you can't get your brain out of Isabella's drawers, but Domenico Barbaja offers you something else you can't resist – money! You receive part of the takings from his operas and his casinos. Together they have turned you into a prostitute, Gioacchino. Isabella the tart, and Gioacchino the prostitute! What a combination!"

Gioacchino leaps to his feet, suddenly, explosively angry. "You've just gone way, way too far, my friend! Who are you to make pronouncements? What have you ever achieved? Answer me! What?"

Maestro lunges forward so that his face is inches from Gioacchino's. He opens his mouth to speak, then closes it, turns away, and starts towards the door.

"Yes! That's right," cries Gioacchino, and he paces the room in anger, "run away! Go on! If that's how it is – if that's how you want it to be – then go! See if it troubles me one gnat's testicle! Go! Go now!"

Maestro moves quickly to the door. "With the greatest of pleasure!" he shouts.

Gioacchino starts to come after him then turns away again. "Don't think I don't know what this is all about, my friend – you are consumed with jealousy!"

"Me jealous? Jealous of what? Of what? Of you and the tart?"

"Because I have the tart, and you don't! Because I am Gioacchino Rossini! Gioacchino, the successful and famous and loved and admired! People pass me in the streets and whisper, loud enough so I can hear, 'That's him! That's Rossini!' They try to touch me – for luck! Me! They try to steal my hat, my kerchief – anything as long as it's mine. Don't tell me you haven't noticed – I've seen your eyes."

"You think I want your brand of cheap adulation, do you? You think I need to be worshipped by beggars and street scum too?"

"Anyone noticing you at all would be remarkable. You live in the dark, in the shadows. No one knows you exist."

Maestro is incandescent. "No one – except kings and queens!"

"Kings and queens?" says Gioacchino in disbelief, and he laughs and laughs, bending over and holding his stomach to show how much he is laughing, "… kings and queens! Maestro – you delude yourself! You don't exist except through me."

"I am … I am …" Maestro stammers.

"What? Who? Who are you?"

"If you knew … if you knew … then you would realise that you are not even worthy of kissing my foot. No one is worthy of kissing my foot!"

"Your foot!" and Gioacchino lays back his head and bays with laughter. "Special, is it? Let's see it then. Come on – hold it up so that I can admire it!" and he rushes at Maestro and tries to grab his foot. Maestro backs away, Gioacchino follows, and they perform a chase-the-foot dance around the room – with Gioacchino grabbing and laughing and Maestro skipping and gasping.

Gioacchino suddenly stops. "No? You can kiss mine if you like!" He flips off his slipper and holds up a foot, "Beautiful foot, don't you think?" He wiggles it. "A foot for kings and queens. You can kiss it if you like …" and he starts to chase Maestro again, but on one leg, trying to wave his foot in Maestro's face as he hops, "Come on, kiss it!"

Maestro turns, bolts out the door and slams it behind him.

He leans back against the corridor wall and closes his eyes, gasping for breath. He turns and stares at the door, then slowly takes out an imaginary pistol from inside his coat. He inserts powder, rams it with the pistol rod, adds shot, rams it, pulls back the hammer and cocks it. He crooks his finger over the trigger and, holding it high in the air in one hand, moves to the door and opens the door with the other hand. He sticks one foot out around the door-frame and wiggles it.

Gioacchino is staring out of the window, rigid, unmoving. He stares at the distant sea, but does not see it. He is sweating. He is shaking. He is crying in anger, in regret, in fury, in shame.

Maestro tips his head around the doorframe so that his foot and head only are showing, and giggles.

Gioacchino turns and stares and laughs and holds out his arms.

They move together and embrace.

"Maestro, Maestro, Maestro," says Gioacchino. "I know you love me, and that is why you said those things, and why I am kissing you and not running you through with my dagger."

"But what I said was unforgivable," insisted Maestro. "I called you a prostitute and that tart of yours a … a …"

"… a tart. Yes, you did. Isabella the tart, you said. It has a ring to it, yes? The Spanish tart … the queen of tarts."

"The Spanish Queen of tarts!" says Maestro, and he is getting excited again. "We could set her to music and make her the most famous tart there has ever been …" and Maestro walks, processes, with his right arm held up high, his wrist loose, and bows, "The Knave of Bologna and his Queen of Tarts!" and he curtsies.

Gioacchino bows to his curtsey, and takes Maestro's outstretched hand. They process together. "You and I. Arm in arm, we can do anything, my friend."

"Then why don't we?" urges Maestro, suddenly all intent, all urgency. "Come away from here, leave Isabella and her tragedies – even if it is only for a few months."

"Months?"

"I must see travel north to Magdalena and the children soon. Come to Rome with me as soon as Otello closes, and we will write an opera the like of which has never yet been seen or heard."

"What do you mean? What opera are you talking about?"

"The opera that Paisiello wrote and missed the point of completely – the comic opera that Figaro …"

"You mean 'The Barber of Seville'!"

"Yes! 'Il Barbiere di Siviglia'. You can do it. I know you can do it. What do you say?"

Gioacchino is excited but torn, "I could get away for a short while – my contract with Barbaja allows me that – but what about Isabella?"

"Balls to Isabella! Now, there's an idea – you could leave your balls behind with her, when you go – I mean, would she notice you had gone, do you think?"

"No," says Gioacchino.

And they both burst out laughing and start hugging and slapping, heady, intoxicated, manic.

THIRTY-NINE

Italy

Isabella's rooms. Naples

Gioacchino and Isabella are lying in bed, side by side, on their backs, both staring at the ceiling.

Isabella sucks in her breath, expels it loudly, and says, quietly, ominously quietly, "And he thinks my voice will be too heavy, too basso, for this 'Barbiere di Siviglia' thing of yours, yes?"

"No, no! Just a little too dramatic, too rich, he thinks."

"Does he now? And what does he suggest?"

"Oh, that we use a nothing voice – you know, a light, tripping, girl voice."

"Such as …?"

"Such as … nobody, really – perhaps … just perhaps … Righetti-Giorgi."

Isabella sits bolt upright, her marvellous, enormous, pendulous breasts swinging and gyrating like pendulums. "Geltrude Righetti-Giorgi! That skinny runt!"

She leaps out of bed and everything goes swinging and gyrating, breasts, belly, buttocks. "Light? Tripping? Light and tripping like a dried-up old cow, you mean? A girl? My God! I cannot believe you are swallowing all this, Gioacchino."

She lunges forward until she is leaning over him, her marvellous breasts swinging dangerously close to his nose, to his eyes, to his mouth. "Maestro hates me!" she hisses. "You know that, don't you? You know the nasty old fart tried to jump into my bath with me. And he hates me because I laughed at him."

"He told me about that," says Gioacchino to the breasts. "He says you misunderstood what he …"

"I misunderstood nothing!" she screams. "What I don't understand is why you haven't defended my honour and killed him!"

Gioacchino gasps and stares at both breasts, mesmerized, unable to look away, unable to think. The nipples are swollen and engorged. Why? Is she sexually excited? Why is she sexually excited?

"If you really loved me," she says, "you'd never see that odious little toad again!" She stands and they swing. "He wants to get you away from me. He wants you for himself. So he can live through you. Through your talent."

"Not fair, Isabella, not fair. Maestro … has brilliant ideas. He often writes arrangements with me. He comes up with some of the most outrageous concepts that …"

And down she swoops again, planting a hand either side of his head, swamping him with her sex, knowing exactly what she is doing. "He's a twisted old man with twisted hands!"

Gioacchino says nothing.

"And how did they get like that? Do you know? Have you ever asked him? Is there anything you actually know about him?"

"Isabella …"

"I warn you, Gioacchino!" she breathes into his face, "you go to Rome with that cripple – that creature – and you will live to regret it!" She comes even closer so that her lips are touching his bare skin, so that he can feel the vibration of the words as well as the sound of them, "I will live to make you regret it!"

FORTY

Italy

Rome

In somewhat grubby, second floor lodgings in Piazza Campo dei Fiori, Rome, in which the host, one Giulio Cesare, and his wife, Claudia, happily fight over everything, morning and night, regardless of who is present or listening to their bickering, Gioacchino and Maestro are writing and eating and talking all at the same time, pouring wine and food into their mouths, so that they spill, and writing on top of the spillings, finishing one another's sentences.

"We go back to the original Beaumarchais play …" says Gioacchino.

"… the irrepressible Figaro, the scheming Bartolo …" adds Maestro.

"… the lovely Rosina, and her bastard of a husband, Almaviva…"

"… in a sumptuous, fiery Spanish setting …"

"… as different from that old fool, Paisiello's version of 'Il Barbiere' as we can make it."

"Oh, we will, my friend, we will!" promises Maestro. "I mean,

I'm sure he only agreed to your writing another 'Barber' because he was convinced you would come up with a resounding and catastrophic flop – after all, what would a twenty-three-year-old boy know about writing opera?"

"What would a twenty-three-year-old boy know about anything? Life, death …"

"… love, women …"

"Now, there is a subject that Gioacchino Rossini has deep and intimate knowledge of, I assure you, my friend – certainly more than a limp old faggot like Paisiello!" He hangs a limp wrist and sings, Baroque style, 'Poor Paisiello!'"

And Maestro joins him in an improvised duet, both with limp, hanging wrists, as they sing, "Poor Paisiello!" complete with such flourishes and embroidery that would have made Paisiello himself proud.

On the outskirts of Rome, a coach lurches and sways along the rutted way approaching the Eternal city from the south. The coach is being pulled by four straining, sweating, tired horses. Isabella is seated in the coach, holding tight to the window frame with both hands. Seated opposite her is a cadaverous, rat-faced man, in black, from head to toe. Carlo. Servant, retainer, thief, cut-throat, at her or anyone else's bidding. Four armed out-riders escort the carriage. Two in front, two behind.

On the stage of Rome's Teatro Argentina, singers are rehearsing. Gioacchino and Maestro are seated at the back of the auditorium, still writing the orchestrations to the opera, still talking, still eating, still drinking.

"Thirteen days, my friend!" says Maestro. "No one is going to believe that we could write 'Il Barbiere di Siviglia' in just thirteen days."

"For generations to come," says Gioacchino, "people will say that Gioacchino Rossini cheated – that he copied whole sections from his earlier operas, that he had an accomplice …"

"An accomplice?" Maestro stops still and looks up at his friend, waiting.

Gioacchino goes on eating and writing, unaware of Maestro's sudden stillness.

"What an absurd idea," says Maestro. "Gioacchino and an accomplice!"

"And tomorrow night," says Gioacchino, "my beloved 'Barbiere' opens."

"Your beloved 'Barbiere' …" Maestro stands. "I'm sorry, Gioacchino, but I have to leave you for a while."

"Leave? Now? Today?"

"Yes, today. I received a letter from my daughter, Therese, last night. Magdalena is not well. I must go to her."

"But why did you wait until now? Why didn't you go last night?"

"Because I had this silly idea that you needed me here – as an accomplice or something equally frivolous." Maestro turns away then turns back momentarily, "I may be back for opening night – but then again, I may not. I wish you well for the première of your beloved 'Barbiere', Gioacchino."

"Maestro! Wait! I didn't mean …"

But Maestro has gone.

Later that same night, in a backstreet across The Eternal City, Isabella Colbran leans in close to speak to the leader of the group of hired men she has brought with her from Naples to provide armed protection on the treacherous roads from Naples to Rome, and for a particular task in Rome itself. "We want the opera destroyed," she hisses. "Totally destroyed. I have asked Paisiello here …"

The leader of the group defers to her companion, "Signore!"

Paisiello nods an acknowledgement.

"… to join us. Paisiello and I," she continues, "in addition to your services in our journey here, are prepared to pay you well, half now, half when you succeed in destroying the opening night. The opera must be a laughing-stock …"

"… hooted and booed from the stage," wheezes Paisiello, "right from the overture."

"… but especially when that cow, Righetti-Giorgi, comes on," adds Isabella.

"And look out for the popinjay, Rossini," adds Paisiello, flecking spit at them in his excitement. "He'll be parading himself near the keyboard in the orchestra pit."

"Oh, we've got something special for Rossini, my dear Paisiello," assures Isabella. "He'll be wearing a hideous Spanish jacket, with huge gold buttons …"

"How do you know he will l be wearing this jacket?" says the claque leader.

"Trust me," says Isabella, "he will be wearing it. Domenico Barbaja gave it to him as a present, especially for opening night." She hands him a purse of money, "Until tomorrow."

The leader opens the purse, pours the coins out into his hand, counts them slowly, much to Isabella's annoyance, then stuffs the purse inside his shirt.

The group disperses, Paisiello and his man one way, the claque another, all staying close to their leader, of course – as he is carrying the money.

Isabella turns to look into the shadows behind her. She signals with her hand. A figure moves forward. Carlo. "Stay as close as you can to Gioacchino, but even closer to Maestro, at all times," she snaps. "Watch them and learn where they eat, where they sleep."

Carlo nods once and moves off after the men.

FORTY-ONE

Italy

Rome

February 10, 1816, and Rome's Teatro Argentina is full to overflowing, buzzing with excitement. The orchestra concludes its tuning up, and the composer, Gioacchino Rossini, wearing a hazel-coloured, Spanish jacket, with two rows of large, gold buttons down the front, enters from the side door and moves to the keyboard. He is greeted immediately with catcalls, laughter, and whistling.

"Eh, Toro!" calls out the claque leader.

This is instantly picked up by other claque members, spread about the theatre, with cries of "Toro!" and "Olé!" and one talented member of the group plays a piercing blast on a trumpet – as they do in the bullfights in Spain.

Gioacchino smiles, in pain, and sits.

The opera begins. Many in the audience talk throughout the overture, moving around and greeting one another like old friends.

Carlo stands in the dim light, against the theatre wall, just behind Gioacchino.

Garcia, the tenor, enters, with his guitar, to accompany himself in a serenade which he has composed himself. He proceeds to tune the instrument in front of the audience. The audience boos and whistles.

Figaro's 'Largo al factotum' and the following duet between Figaro and the Count are drowned out under a barrage of whistles and shouting.

Vitarelli, playing Basilio, trips on a trap door as he crosses the stage, and cuts his face badly. He staggers off to raucous laughter.

Righetti-Giorgi makes her entrance as Rosina. The claque members roar with disapproval and make cow mooing sounds and ring a cowbell, to greet her. She sings her cavatina, 'Una voce poco fa'. Some in the audience applaud and the barracking subsides momentarily.

A cat wanders on stage during the finale to Act One. Zamboni chases the cat off-stage, but it reappears from the opposite side and Botticelli, playing Bartolo, attempts, unsuccessfully, to catch it. The audience cheers the cat on and encourages it with loud miaowing. The cat wins and Botticelli gives up.

The first Act mercifully ends. Gioacchino stands and applauds his cast for enduring the insults and abuse of the audience. However, the audience mistakes his actions and motives, and assumes he is applauding his own opera. Led by the eager claque members, they shout and hiss their disapproval. Gioacchino immediately leaves the pit and the theatre, and goes back to his hotel, leaving the cast to their own devices.

FORTY-TWO

Italy

Pianoro

Magdalena is sitting up in bed, propped by cushions.

Maestro enters with a bowl, spoon and serviette. He sits next to her and feeds her, spoonful by spoonful. Magdalena finally signals 'enough'. Maestro wipes her mouth with the serviette, then lays bowl, spoon and serviette down.

Magdalena takes hold of his hands, turns them up, exposing the scars in his palms. She kisses each scar in turn. Maestro takes her head in his hands and turns it gently to the side, exposing the scars on her neck and face. He leans forward and kisses each scar, separately, tenderly.

Magdalena stretches up and holds his head so that he is looking at her. "We have had such a life, my love, such a life."

"And will, for many years to come," he says.

"Perhaps. But promise me – if not for your own sake, then for my sake, and for your son and daughter's sake – you will show restraint. You will stay in the shadows."

Maestro nods. "As I do always, my love. I am a spectre, a phantom, an apparition…"

"Oh yes… but you left out 'teller of tales', and 'romancer', my love. But I love you for it. All I ask is that you are careful."

"I know… but I must return south soon. 'Il Barbiere di Siviglia' opens tonight in Rome and I should be there with Gioacchino."

"I know, I know. Leave early tomorrow morning. Therese comes to me every day now – she and Alberto are very happy together – and they have no baby yet, so she can look after me. Now, lie next to me until I sleep, my love."

FORTY-THREE

Italy

Rome

The day after the opening night disaster, Gioacchino returns to the theatre late in the afternoon, and summons the tenor, Garcia.

"You will sing what I write for you to sing, Garcia," he says. "You will sing 'Ecco ridente in cielo' as Almaviva's serenade, and not your own Spanish guitar confection! You will not tune or play with your instrument on-stage …"

There is a loud guffaw from the back of the theatre from the Impresario.

Gioacchino glares at him then turns back to Garcia. "Don't even touch your instrument …"

There is an even louder guffaw from the theatre Impresario, who turns, convulsing, and exits.

"You will sing with the orchestra!" shouts Gioacchino. "I am going back to my hotel. Tell the others I said, 'Toi! Toi! Toi! for tonight."

"You are not staying to speak to them?" says Garcia, in disbelief.

"No, I am not staying," says Gioacchino. "Tell them I am ill," and he exits hurriedly.

Later that same night, Gioacchino is sleeping peacefully in his hotel, but his well-earned sleep is broken when he is awoken by an uproar from outside, from the street below. He crosses to the window and sees a large, noisy crowd below his very window, carrying torches, and shouting, demanding to be admitted.

"They're going to set the building on fire!" breathes Gioacchino and he quickly pulls a pair of breeches up over his night-shirt, and hurries down the back stairs. He exits into the stables beneath the hotel, and hides in the straw amongst the neighing, disturbed horses.

A black-clad figure has been watching him enter the stables. The figure now creeps from stall to stall, then calls out, "Gioacchino! Gioacchino Rossini! Where are you?"

Gioacchino nestles down further and pulls straw over his head, disturbing the horse whose stall he is in, and it rears and neighs.

The figure comes close to investigate. "Gioacchino! Is that you? Are you there?"

Gioacchino does not answer.

"It's me, Garcia, your favourite tenor! I saw you come down the back stairs."

Gioacchino's head emerges from the straw. "Why are you hounding me? What do you want?"

"You! We want you! Listen to the shouts, Gioacchino – they are saying 'Bravo! Bravo maestro!' It was a huge success tonight! You should have heard me. I was magnificent. The audience loved me – and 'Il

Barbiere' of course! The street is full of people, maestro. They want to congratulate you!"

"Shit on them and their bravos! I'm not going out there for love or money," and he ducks past Garcia and flees back up the hotel stairs to his room.

The crowd out front is milling around, drinking and laughing and swearing – and getting tired of standing out in the cold. Maestro appears amongst them. Carlo stands close.

Garcia appears from around the side of the hotel.

"Well, Garcia," cries Maestro, "where is our great composer?"

"He won't come out," says Garcia.

"But did you tell him what a triumph it was tonight?"

"I did."

"And what did he say?" yells a man in the crowd.

"He said, 'Shit on them and their bravos!'"

"Shit on them …" says the same man but the rest of his words are lost in the shouts of anger from the crowd. Someone throws an orange at Garcia, as the bearer of the insult. The orange hits him in the eye. He staggers. The crowd starts to turn ugly.

"My friends! My friends!" shouts Maestro. "Calm yourselves. Garcia must have misheard. Wait! I will go and speak to him." And he quickly disappears around the side of the building.

The hotel proprietor rushes into Gioacchino's bedroom with Maestro at his side.

Gioacchino is lying in bed, with the sheets pulled up high, under his chin.

"I beg you, I beg you, sir!" cries the proprietor, "If you don't come down, they'll set fire to my hotel!"

There is a crash of glass as two of Gioacchino's windows are broken by flying missiles.

"Aaah!" cries Gioacchino. "I'm not going near that rabble!"

"If you won't come down, my friend," says Maestro, "then I beg you allow me to bring one or two up here so that they can congratulate you and shake your hand – that's all they want, I assure you."

Gioacchino lowers the sheet from his face. "That's all they want? Are you sure?"

Maestro and the hotel proprietor both nod their heads furiously. "Right, so be it," says Gioacchino. "But only a few, mind you, and pick pretty ones while you're at it."

"Right, my friend, only the ones with big tits." And Maestro and a greatly relieved Hotel Proprietor, quickly exit.

While they are gone, Gioacchino clambers out from under the covers, dashes to a set of drawers, searches quickly and finally finds a pistol. He dashes back to the bed, places the pistol under his sheets, takes it out again and cocks it, places it back again, and climbs into bed. He pulls the sheets high up under his chin again.

Maestro enters the room with ten or twelve dignitaries and members of the cast, including four young women, two of whom have enormous breasts, plus the black-eyed Garcia, and, in the background, a silent Carlo. They call out "Bravo!" and "Bravo, maestro!" and "Magnifico!" as they enter. They each shake Gioacchino's hand, including Carlo, while all the time Gioacchino stays in bed, with the sheets tucked firmly up under his chin, holding out his hand to be shaken, then returning it quickly under the sheets and the pillow, to the pistol.

FORTY-FOUR

Italy

Gioacchino's rooms. Naples

Gioacchino opens his front door to find Isabella standing there in an outrageously gorgeous outfit, complete with feather boa and feather hat. Her eyes are closed, her arms are open, waiting to be kissed. She is a step down from Gioacchino, so this is totally feasible. Gioacchino embraces her. She does not respond, she accepts his embrace, as if it is her due, opens her eyes and steps inside.

"Welcome back to Naples, Gioacchino," she says.

Clearly I'm no longer her little Gioacchi-Woacchi, thinks Gioacchino.

"And how was it? How was your little opera? "The Barber", wasn't it?"

"… of Seville! Yes! Wonderful! Wonderful!"

"Oh, I'm so glad. No problems at all then?"

"No, no, none," gushes Gioacchino, "… there was a spot of bother on the first night – rival opera houses, jealous composers – you know the way it is – but after that, wonderful reception."

"Isn't that just divine? I am so happy for you. I knew it would be a success, of course – I was telling Domenico what a success it was going to be only last week." She gives Gioacchino a quick pat on the top of his head for being such a good little boy, and takes his hand. She sits on a sofa and drags him down next to her. "Right, you and I need to talk – an intimate little discussion, you might say. Where is the toad?"

"The toad?"

"Don't play games, please, Gioacchino, it's so tiresome. You know exactly who I mean."

"I'm sure I don't …"

"Gioacchino!" she snaps.

"Maestro has just gone to the market – but he and I have been working flat out …" he says.

"Of course you have!" she says.

"… on a new opera."

"A new opera! Domenico will be so pleased! He's been at his wit's end – I've had to console him, almost every day, poor lamb, and nights too, you can imagine…"

"Yes, our dere fiend will be pleased …" he pauses, expecting her to laugh at the joke, but she does not laugh. "Yes, an opera … with a role – such a role, my dear Isabella, the likes of which the world has never seen! It is Cenerentola!"

"Isn't that nice."

"And it's for you, dearest. Without you, the opera wouldn't exist. You are Cinderella, of course. The role demands a singer with a three-octave voice range, an actor of extraordinary theatrical ability … a woman with the voice of an angel – all of which is you, my love!"

"I'm sure. Now, as I said, we need to talk …"

Maestro is strolling the crowded streets of Naples, enjoying the bustle, the noise, the smells of the filthy, marvellous town that it is, and approaches Gioacchino's rooms and looks up at the third floor to see Gioacchino's door suddenly open, and Isabella emerge, closely attended by Gioacchino. They stop on the landing. They kiss and embrace, Gioacchino straining on tiptoe to reach her, Isabella bending to accommodate him. Like mother and child, only not at all like mother and child.

Maestro pulls back into an alley and watches, and rolls out his favourite cannon. He points the cannon in the direction of Isabella, elevates it a little more to allow for the third-floor height, pours in powder, rams it home, picks up a cannonball, staggers with the weight of it, inserts it, with difficulty, into the muzzle, rams it home, then squints along the barrel to make sure it is on target. He nudges it and adjusts the elevation a fraction again.

Isabella turns to come down the stairs.

Maestro lights a taper with a flintlock, touches it to the fuse and is thrown backwards by the recoil of the explosion. He peers through the smoke to see a perfectly round cannonball hole in the middle of Isabella's body, fitting exactly between fanny and tits, so that he can see the wall and part of the door beyond. Maestro is very pleased with himself. It is the shot of a master marksman.

Escorted by Gioacchino, Isabella descends the stairs to the ground and gets into a waiting carriage, clearly unaware of the gaping hole in her midriff. Gioacchino closes the carriage door and kisses her again through the carriage window. Poor thing. The carriage drives off. Gioacchino goes back into his rooms.

Maestro waits until the carriage has disappeared then climbs the stairs and follows Gioacchino inside. "Very touching scene, my dear Gioacchino."

"You saw?" says Gioacchino.

"I couldn't help but see – as did half of Naples."

"Congratulations are in order, my friend."

"Why congratulations?"

"Because I have just asked Isabella to marry me, and she has graciously accepted."

"You what? Are you mad?"

"Am I mad?"

"She's seven years older than you."

"When you are in love, what does age matter?"

"But she's a beautiful woman!"

"Hah? I didn't realise beauty was a failing in a woman."

"But that's where you are wrong, my friend. It is! You are not experienced in the ways of women. Beauty like hers is the last quality you want in a woman."

"Now who's the madman?"

"Marry a sow, Gioacchino. Marry a pig of a woman and be happy for the rest of your life."

Gioacchino bursts out laughing.

189

Maestro is not to be side-tracked. "A sow will love you, look after you, cook for you," he says. "She is not going to mind when you wander and stay out at night, and, the most important aspect of all – she's never going to cheat on you – because what man is going to want to bed a sow?"

Gioacchino is still laughing. "You are outrageous, my friend! I have no intention of marrying a sow!"

"But why marry at all? You can have that woman now whenever you like. You can poke her fire every night without ever having to pay for the wood. Free. The best way. The only way. Why marry and spoil it all?"

"Because … because I choose to."

"But why, for God's sake?"

"Because I love her … and, because she owns a villa in Castenaso, extensive lands in Sicily, and has forty thousand scudi in cash."

"Aha!" cries Maestro, "so that is why you are marrying. Now we have it!"

"No, now I have it – or I soon will!" rejoins Gioacchino. We eke out a living, you and I. We survive. But now we won't have to scrape by on pennies. I won't be rich, well, maybe a little rich, but I will survive, comfortably – and we can write, my friend. For the first time in our lives we will be able to write without fear, without looking over our shoulders for the debt collectors. Do you know how that feels, Maestro?"

"Yes, my friend, I do," says Maestro, and for the first time, Maestro is subdued.

Magdalena is lying in bed. Her doctor is leaning over her, holding a potion to her lips. Magdalena drinks it with difficulty and spills some down her night attire. She coughs, and coughs, and has to swallow hard to hold the coughing back.

"Where is your husband?" the doctor asks.

"In the South. Why?"

"Send for him."

"I do not want to disturb his work... it is important to him... he will be home soon."

"Send for him now."

Magdalena looks at him for a long time, sighs, heaves up onto an elbow, with difficulty, and calls, "Therese!"

Therese comes hurrying out of the kitchen to stand at Magdalena's side.

"I want... I want you to write a letter for me, Therese..." says Magdalena.

FORTY-FIVE

Italy

Naples

Maestro, his clothes in disarray, is hurrying down the street towards Gioacchino's rooms. Maestro is carrying an opened letter in his hand. He races up the stairs and bursts into Gioacchino's rooms without knocking and closes immediately on Gioacchino at the piano. Isabella is standing next to him, her hand on the piano.

Maestro speaks to Gioacchino and only to him. "Magdalena is gravely ill … she may be dying. I must go north."

Gioacchino stands. "Go! Do you want me to come with you?"

"No, I'll travel faster alone – and I don't know how long…" he cannot finish.

"Go! Just go, my friend!" urges Gioacchino.

They embrace, and Maestro turns and leaves.

Isabella has not made a sound, or spoken a word, while Maestro was in the room.

There is a long silence, then Isabella calls, "Gabriella!"

Gabriella enters from the back room.

"Go to my lodgings, Gabriella, and pack for a journey. We will be away for some time."

Gioacchino turns to stare at Isabella. She ignores him.

"And pull out the trunk from my dressing-room that we filled some time ago …"

"You mean the one with the …"

"You know the one. I'll be along later. And tell Carlo I wish to see him urgently. Hurry now."

Gabriella leaves.

"What are you doing? You heard Maestro. He wishes to travel alone. It's a family matter …"

"Oh, this has nothing to do with your dear old Maestro, Gioacchino. We are not going to Magdalena. We are going to my villa in Castenaso. I will get word to my mother and father to meet us there, and, we will be married."

"Married? Just like that?"

"Yes, just like that. Do you have a problem with that, Gioacchino?"

"No, not a problem as such … except, I thought you would want an occasion of a wedding, a society wedding. I mean, people … friends here will miss it."

"You mean Maestro."

"Not only Maestro… Domenico as well."

"Domenico? After what he did to you over 'Otello', you would want Domenico at our wedding? The important people will be there, won't they? You and I. What else matters?"

Isabella waits impatiently until Gioacchino has left the room then she signals Carlo to come close. He does so. Too close. She waves him further away and puts a handkerchief to her nose.

"Maestro is leaving today to go north," she says through her handkerchief. "To his home. Follow him. Wherever he goes. I want to know where he lives, who he sees, where he comes from – everything, you understand?"

Carlo nods.

Isabella hands him a purse of money. "Report to me when you have something and there will be more. Now, move quickly."

Carlo leaves immediately.

FORTY-SIX

Italy

Naples

"Sorry, we're full," says the driver, and he turns away, climbs up onto the carriage and takes up the reins.

"But I must get to Rome as soon as possible," argues Maestro, "my wife is ill, desperately ill."

"Buy a horse then and ride!" shouts the driver and he separates the reins so that one hand controls the front two horses and the other the back two.

"I don't have time to find a horse," screams Maestro, "and a lone rider won't survive on this road! Please!"

The driver looks down at him, then flicks his head towards the rear, "Climb up on top with the luggage then – there's probably room for one more."

"Thank you! Thank you!" cries Maestro and he clambers up the side netting onto the roof of the carriage.

"And don't fall off! 'Cos we won't be stopping to pick you up!" shouts the driver." He snickers at the horses, jiggles the reins, and they're off with a jerk.

Maestro holds on tight to the netting and forces himself down between the bags, creating a hole that he can slip into and which will give him support.

And it starts to rain.

Maestro pulls his hat down lower over his face and closes his eyes.

Behind the lumbering carriage is a man on a bony, dun horse. He digs in his heels and the horse trots after the carriage, closes to a distance where it protects the man from some of the rain, then maintains the gap. Carlo.

They travel through the Neapolitan countryside without incident, thanks to the soldiers every couple of kilometres, and the cleared shrubbery, and don't stop until early evening where they pull into an inn, eat, sleep fitfully, then continue, early the next morning. Carriage and horse.

They enter the Papal territories and tension rises in everyone as the soldiers disappear and the trees and bushes close in.

But all is well all day, and everyone's spirits rise as they approach Terracina. Then there is a loud shout up ahead. Maestro pops his head up over the luggage and sees four men on horseback blocking the trail. The men are brandishing pistols in the air. The carriage slows.

Maestro hugs the luggage and, keeping as low as he can, carefully climbs down the netting. As soon as the carriage stops, he drops to the ground, scuttles low into the trees, crouches, remains still for a moment, then slips from tree to tree, away from the trail and the carriage and the shouting. He circles in a wide arc away from the trail then keeps moving northward, always northward.

And behind him, at a discreet distance, comes a man, dressed in black, on a bony dun horse.

Some hours later, Maestro walks into the Inn at Terracina. Fabio's wife sees him first and calls Fabio. They embrace, and Fabio tells him that the carriage had arrived a hour before, full of the news of the hold-up, how they'd stood their ground, been prepared to fight, but in the end, took the safer course and handed over some, but not all, of their money and jewellery.

They'd booked the bedrooms, of course, and so Fabio offers to set up a pallet of straw on the dining room floor for Maestro, which Maestro gratefully accepts.

There is no sign of the lone rider and his dun horse.

They eat a simple meal together, and reminisce, and Maestro explains why he is travelling north on his own, and the urgency.

The carriage leaves again early the following morning, and the black rider and dun horse suddenly appear behind them again.

They travel without further incident to Rome, where Maestro changes carriage and secures an inside seat this time to Bologna. The shadow follows at a distance.

In Bologna, Maestro is forced to hire a horse to ride to Pianoro. Carlo listens closely as Maestro negotiates the hireage and to Maestro's saying that he is unable to specify the day or date when he will return the horse, but he will return it. This will cost more, says the owner. So be it, says Maestro. Maestro buys provisions for the journey, including food, drink, a bell, and a blanket, and he sets off northwest. With the shadow following. The shadow has to be even more circumspect now however, without the distraction of a carriage. In fact, it is so difficult, and the likelihood that he will soon be discovered by Maestro, causes Carlo to pass Maestro, giving him a wide berth, and head for Pianoro independently, with the intention of waiting on the outskirts of the town until Maestro arrives from the south-east, and then falling in behind again.

And so it comes to pass.

FORTY-SEVEN

Italy

Maestro's home in Pianoro

Magdalena is lying in bed. She is gravely ill. Her eyes are closed. Her breathing is short and shallow. Maestro is sitting on the bed next to her. He is holding her hand and crying silently.

Magdalena opens her eyes and smiles weakly at him. "Don't cry, my love …" she breathes, "… it's time."

"I won't let you," answers Maestro.

"There's nothing you can do, my love."

"There is!" cries Maestro, desperately jovial. "I can find another body – and put it in your place – it worked for me, didn't it? Look here I am – thirty years later …"

"Make it a young body then, my love. A pretty one …"

"With golden hair and forget-me-not blue eyes …"

"… and no scars – perfect face and neck – as I was before."

"You don't have scars, Magdalena. You never did, to me."

"And you were always the blind one, my love … play me

something."

"Play?" he says.

"Yes ... Eine kleine ..."

And Maestro moves to the harpsichord across the room and begins to play "Eine kleine Nachtmusik". Magdalena watches him. He plays it tenderly and beautifully, rising steadily in volume and intensity as he becomes engrossed in the music.

A single, black-plumed horse pulls a cart down a tree-lined path in the mist of a morning. The cart has a coffin on it. The cart is followed closely by four mourners – Maestro, Therese and her new husband, Angelo, and Franz. The procession moves slowly along the path, and disappears into the mist.

FORTY-EIGHT

Italy

Isabella's villa in Castenaso

Isabella and Gioacchino sit on a stone bench together in the garden of her villa. Pink wisteria hangs from a trellis above them, framing them, as in a pose, but there is no one to see them. Isabella is breathtakingly beautiful in a white bridal gown and headdress that contrasts stunningly with her raven-black, garlanded hair. Gioacchino had had great difficulty finding suitable dress attire for a short bridegroom, but with Gabriella's skill with scissors and needle, he looks appropriate, if a little underdone, compared to his wife-to-be.

Isabella takes Gioacchino's hand in hers. "For once, for once, my dear Gioacchino, I have you to myself," she breathes, *dolce voce*.

"We are often alone, my love," smiles Gioacchino.

"Just you and me – without a shadow lurking there behind you."

"You mean Maestro."

"If you say so, my dear. It's all very fortunate really, isn't it?"

"What is?"

"When it's raining in one place, the sun is shining somewhere else. And it's shining on us, right now, isn't it, my love?"

Out of the house come a small, strange collection of people – a priest, Isabella's mother and father, Gabriella, the maid, who is to be a witness, and a peasant from the estate, Luigi, who is to be the other witness. Luigi has been commandeered from the fields to attend by Isabella, despite the fact that Luigi has no shoes, is dressed in a smock, smells of garlic and cheap wine, and cannot read. Needs must.

Isabella stands, waits for Gioacchino to hold out his arm, rests her hand on his when he eventually realizes what she is waiting for, and they move forward to meet the others. They stop in front of the priest. The others fall in behind – mother and father, beaming, Gabriella, willing that they can soon get out of the burning sun, and Luigi, behind, scowling.

The priest crosses himself, and begins …

FORTY-NINE

Italy

Maestro's home in Pianoro

Maestro settles affairs in Pianoro. Therese's husband is a local vintner, with his own house bequeathed to him by his parents before they died. He and Therese live together in the house and tend the vines. It is decided that Franz will live with them and help with the harvest and wine-making. Maestro's house will be left empty in the meantime, in case Maestro decides to return to Pianoro.

Maestro leaves a few days later via Bologna where he returns the horse, takes a carriage from Bologna to Rome, then a carriage south to Terracina.

Without a shadow.

At the inn, he meets with his friend, eats, drinks, sleeps, and asks an unexpected question of his host.

"On my trip from the south," says Maestro, "I noticed a mule, tethered out back. Does that belong to you, Fabio?"

"Indeed it does, and a more willing and gentle creature you could not imagine. Why?"

"Can I hire it?"

"Hire it? Yes, of course, you can. Her name is Francesca, by the way, after my wife. "And he roars with laughter. When he has control of himself again, he asks, "But why would you want to hire a mule? A carriage is much faster and certainly more comfortable."

"But much more dangerous, my friend. You may recall, the last carriage I travelled the road south of Terracina, the carriage was stopped and the passengers robbed – and could have been killed, of course, if the robbers had had a mind to it."

"But riding a mule means you will be travelling on your own – easy pickings for even one little bandito!"

"I have a plan – and don't ask, my friend, because I will not tell you now. If I survive, I will tell you all when I return Francesca to you. Trust me."

The next morning the carriage departs without Maestro. Maestro gathers his few possessions, is introduced to Francesca, sits on Francesca, and trots off southwards, with an intrigued but trusting Fabio waving them both arrivederci.

About four or five kilometres on the notorious Appian Way, south of Terracina, Maestro and Francesca are confronted by two banditi, who are laughing as they step out into his path. They stop in the middle of the way, plant their feet square on the ground, hands on hips, and hold up their hands. Probably the most casual and contemptuous robbery that this road has ever seen.

Maestro lifts a leg over the mule's back, steps off, and hunches over. He displays one scarred hand outward-facing in the air, then the other, and reaches into his tunic, takes out his bell and rings it, loudly and clearly.

"Unclean! Unclean!" he calls out to his attackers, and steps forward in a pain-filled shuffle towards them.

Lo banditi stare and go pale. Without speaking, they back away without taking their eyes him, then turn and run for it.

Maestro straightens, pats Francesca on the head, says, "Well done, Francesca!" and climbs onto her back. He tucks his bell into his tunic, lets out a wailing, baying laugh, taps his heels into Francesca's flank, and they are away, Naples-bound.

FIFTY

Italy

A caffè in Naples

"They didn't even invite me to the fucking wedding! Can you believe it?" cries Domenico,

"They didn't invite me either," says Maestro, "in fact, Isabella made sure it happened while I was away."

"... after all I've done for him – my theatres, my money, my free board, my friendship, yes, my friendship – and his response? He flirts with her in front of me, he writes her into all his operas, he fucks her in my dressing-room..." cries Domenico.

"... in your dressing-room?" says Maestro. "He didn't tell me that," and he smiles and shakes his head in admiration.

"... in my theatre, while I'm standing outside the door – I can still hear them at it, grunting and slurping... now, do not misunderstand me, Maestro – I expect this – this is what you do – this is what I do – but to marry her... to run away and marry her, in secret!"

"I think you'll find that she was the one who ran away and married him in secret, my friend."

"She is thirty-seven years old…"

"And he has just turned thirty… born on February twenty ninth, you know – a Leap Year baby, so, in real birthdays, he is actually seven years old," and Maestro lets out a baying, wail of laughter that the caffè clientèle has so gotten used to by this time that they stop reacting with alarm and surprise, as if it is an everyday occurrence.

"And, she is near the end of her child-bearing years…"

"… that's overstating it a little, I think, my friend – and I'm not sure if Gioacchino is that keen to have children anyway…"

"Why didn't they… all right, she… want us there at the wedding then? You tell me."

"I have no answer – except to repeat that this is her doing – not Gioacchino's."

"I mean… Luigi, a local gardener, a bare-footed peasant, dressed in a smock, and stinking of garlic and cheap wine, was a witness at the wedding! But not Impresario Domenico Barbaja! Oh, no! Not good enough! Not wanted. Too guilty, the pair of them."

"It sounds to me, my friend, that you still want her…"

"Me? Want Isabella? No, no, no, my friend. I've already replaced her with a younger version, contralto Teresa Cecconi. You have seen her? Much younger, oh yes…"

"So, what are you really seeking now?" asks Maestro.

"Revenge."

"Revenge? But why?"

"Because they have humiliated me. My friends, my singers, my public, the king, no less, saw her with me. She was my companion, on my arm. And now, she has married my composer, in secret. They have made a fool of Impresario Barbaja. And no one makes a fool of Impresario Barbaja!"

"So how will you exact this vengeance?"

"Simple. My professional relationship with Gioacchino Rossini is over. The free tenancy he has enjoyed in my palazzo in Naples is also over. He will have to find a new little love nest for himself and his bride… and it won't be in Naples. I leave for Milan in a few days – I have been asked to manage La Scala, yes, La Scala no less, by people who value me – my abilities, my experience, my money…"

"My congratulations Impresario! So they are not in Naples at the moment? I have only just returned. I have not seen them."

"No, no, they are in Paris, doing a production of 'Il Viaggio a Reims' at Le Théâtre-Italien – don't worry – this was agreed to long ago, long before the betrayal…"

"So, they are in Paris, on honeymoon…" says Maestro.

"Yes, on honeymoon… but soon to have a rude shock – I have written to Signor and Signorina Rossini at Le Théâtre-Italien informing them of the changes to our little relationship."

"When you say you have written, Impresario… do you that you have written, personally I mean, or via your man, Nicolo?"

"Nicolo. Why do you ask?"

"Oh, no reason, my dere fiend."

"'Dere fiend'? What is this?"

"Just something my good friend Gioacchino and I say sometimes – you know what musicians are like."

"No, not really. You are a strange man, Maestro."

"Yes, I am, aren't I?"

"So... even if you defend your Gioacchino so faithfully, what will you do about Isabella? Because she is now your problem, not mine."

"I will think on it – a privilege of the old, yes? Arrivederci, Impresario Barbaja. We may not meet again."

"Oh, I think we will, Maestro. Arrivederci!"

Maestro sleeps in Naples that night, his final night in that famed city, and the following morning gathers all his belongings together, as few as they are, and sets off for Paris. He returns Francesca to Fabio in Terracina, with kisses – to Francesca of course – takes a carriage to Rome, decides that the Alps and their hazards are too much, so books a passage by ship from Civitavecchia, Rome's seaport, to Marseilles, and then travelling by carriage, in a so solidly built French Diligence carriage, and drawn by four stout horses, regularly changed, through France, and arrives finally in Paris.

Part Seven

FIFTY-ONE

France

Le Théâtre-Italien. Paris

Gioacchino and Isabella are standing close together side-stage. Gioacchino is holding a manuscript of his "Il Viaggio a Reims", so that they can both see it at the same time.

"We'll go from here." He stabs a finger onto the score. "I'll get Gaston to play the introduction, and then you enter, anxious, looking for the priest, yes?"

Isabella turns her eyes to the heavens. "Yes, Gioacchino."

"Good," says Gioacchino and he climbs down over the front of the stage and moves to the back of the auditorium and sits.

"Yes!" he calls.

Gaston strikes a chord on the harpsichord. Isabella walks onto the stage and strikes a pose, facing part up-stage, ready to sing. Gaston begins.

A voice comes out of the dark behind Gioacchino. "She died, Gioacchino."

Gioacchino spins around. "What?"

Maestro stands and moves to Gioacchino. "Magdalena died. I nursed her as best I could, but in the end, I could do nothing."

Gioacchino embraces him. "Oh, my friend, my dear, dear friend. I am so sorry."

"I loved her so much, Gioacchino. And I feel ... no, I know, she loved me."

"Of course she did."

"And she loved your operas, my friend."

"She saw them?"

"All of them. Believe it or not, 'La Pietra' was her favourite."

"It is one of mine."

"Enough of me, Gioacchino. Did you receive Barbaja's letter?

"From our dere fiend? Yes, Isabella and I are arranging for our things to be shipped north. It is for the best."

"Oh, I agree. Our dere fiend is not best pleased. In fact, I'd say he is totally pissed off. While he appreciates your talent, Gioacchino, he does not appreciate your running off and marrying his former lover, thus making him look like a cuckold, and, the final straw, it seems, is that you didn't invite him to the cuckolding wedding. Lovely word that, 'cuckold', isn't it? Says everything. So, you can safely assume he is no longer your dere fiend, my friend."

"Isabella and I are very happy with that state of affairs."

"Is she? Hmm... so, what have you been doing while I have been away, Gioacchino?"

"Just a few minor pieces. But, my friend, I have a story – I was waiting for your return.

"A story?"

"Such a story – a Swiss patriot – William Tell."

"William Tell! I've heard of …"

And at that exact moment, Isabella, who has been singing on stage all this time, over their subdued voices, reaches for and misses a top note. She is clearly flat.

And a startled Maestro, involuntarily, lets out his unmistakable baying laugh.

Isabella and the pianist stop dead. Isabella turns and glares out into the blackness of the auditorium and whispers, with loathing, "The cripple!"

But Maestro's eyes suddenly have a new sparkle in them. "Yes!" he breathes quietly, to himself, "yes!"

FIFTY-TWO

France

A street in Paris

Isabella is staring through a patisserie window at delicacies she dare not eat. Carlo is facing the same window, but far enough away from her.

"His wife died nearly two weeks ago in Pianoro," Carlo is saying. "Her name was …"

"Magdalena – I know her name!" says Isabella crossly.

Carlo stares straight ahead. "The funeral was private – a priest, their daughter and her new husband, their son, and Maestro. No one else."

"Interesting."

"He owns a house in the countryside. Empty. No housekeeper. Here, he eats at the same restaurant in Paris, every day – in the Rue de Rivoli. I can show you both, if you…"

"Yes, yes, later …"

And as the Milanese say, 'Così è la vita!' Such is life. While Isabella is busy plotting Maestro's destruction, Maestro has a few thoughts of his own.

Maestro makes a special trip to Milan, to see Barbaja, and Barbaja gloats, of course, as soon as they meet. "Sooner than I expected, my friend," he says, loving every second of it.

"You were right, I acknowledge, but I thought you should hear my news, in person."

"Tell me."

"There is a glimmer of hope, perhaps more than a glimmer, and that may in part depend on you. Our mutual friend of the female kind has a problem, a significant problem – in fact, I'd go so far as to say a fucking enormous problem!" And he stops, enjoying the moment, enjoying the suspense, even enjoying tormenting Barbaja.

"What?" demands Barbaja.

"Her voice," he whispers. "Her greatest asset for Gioacchino – apart from her money and her enormous buttocks and breasts, of course – is her voice. This is one of the main reasons why he married her in the first place! And she is losing it! She is flat on some of her top notes – and that's the beauty of it – the worst kind of flat – just-under flat, not a tone flat, not even half a tone flat, just enough flat to make your skin crawl. And she knows it, of course, so she compensates by mentally pitching what she thinks is a danger note, a little higher, to make sure, and ends up sharp! Yes! It is wonderful! You sit and you listen and you don't know when it is going to happen. You are on the edge of your seat! You hold your breath! And then… it comes… it comes…"

"Every singer has an off night…"

"No! No! No! I am…" and he stops himself just in time. He starts again, "Think about it, my friend! Gioacchino wrote all the lead roles – Elisabetta, Cenerentola, Desdemona… for that voice. We wrote whole operas for that voice. For that three-octave range voice. She is, after all, the soprano sfogato, is she not? And now, now that voice is suspect! That voice is unsafe. The death knell is tolling, my friend. I hear it. Audiences hear it. And, most important of all, Gioacchino hears it."

"So, what do we do?"

"I know what I am going to do, my friend. We are writing a new opera, Semiramide, right at this moment. And I think there may be, just may be, a few challenging notes in the score for our soprano sfogato. Now, do you have anyone in your company, your list of singers who could stand in – who could sing a demanding coloratura role – in an emergency, Domenico?"

"I do. And when I meet with our mutual friend of the male kind – we do still communicate occasionally, by the way, because of past contracts and future productions – I could perhaps make a few suggestions…"

FIFTY-THREE

France

Gioacchino and Isabella's apartment. Paris

Gioacchino is pacing, stopping, turning, then pacing again. Isabella sits and waits. He obviously has something he wants to say to her, but she has not the slightest intention of helping him.

"Isabella," he says finally, from behind the chaise longue, "I've decided ... after much thought ... to use someone else to sing Semiramide at the Paris Opera."

"You've decided what?" cries Isabella, in complete shock.

Gioacchino has gone visibly pale. "You're ... you're not singing at your best at the moment, my love, and I thought that a little rest... at Castenaso perhaps ..."

Isabella stands. "A rest? Am I hearing correctly? Am I? Have I gone mad – or have you gone mad? I sing one note a little flat. I don't feel well and sing one little note just slightly under pitch... I was stressed... I was tired ..."

"It's ... it's not just one little note, Isabella. I'm afraid there have been many little notes lately. People are starting to say your voice isn't what it was …"

"It's a lie!" and she is screaming now. "It's simply not true! I am singing as well today as I ever did – no, better!" She moves to close with him behind the chaise longue. He circles away, keeping it between them. "Who's put you up to this?" she demands. "Come on, who are these people you keep talking about? You wouldn't have the balls to come up with this on your own. Someone has …" and she spits it out… "the cripple! It's the cripple, isn't it? He put you up to it, didn't he?"

"Maestro has just mentioned a few little …" He circles again.

"I knew it! I knew it! That man is evil! He's the devil himself!" and she stops in her tracks. "Who?"

"Who what?"

"What tart, which one of your mistresses, have you cast in my role?"

"She isn't my mistress. She's a very popular French diva…"

"Who?" she screams, and she's coming at him again.

"… Fodor-Mainvielle. Madame Josephine Fodor-Mainvielle." Circling. Circling.

"The Parisian prostitute!"

"Isabella!" protests Gioacchino.

"What a pair!" she screeches, "A Parisian prostitute and a cripple!"

Gioacchino backs out towards the door.

"Where do you think you are going?" This in a whispering voice that is far, far more frightening than the screams.

Gioacchino stares at her and continues to back away.

"You will not walk away from me when I am talking to you!"

Gioacchino reaches the door and yanks it open.

"You will not go out that door!"

Gioacchino bolts out the door and slams it shut behind him.

There is silence.

And then, as huge, fat, hot tears start to roll down Isabella's beautiful, almost flawless face, she whispers, "You will come back right now, do you hear me?"

FIFTY-FOUR

France

A theatre dressing-room at Paris Opera. Paris

Isabella enters the dressing-room at Paris Opera. Madame Fodor-Mainvielle is seated, adding finishing touches to her make-up.

"Josephine darling!" cries Isabella.

"Isabella darling!" cries Josephine.

They kiss one another on both cheeks.

Isabella holds up a bottle of Champagne from an already opened bottle, and pours the contents into one of two glasses that she is carrying, "Just a little something to celebrate your first night!" she gushes, and offers the now filled glass to Fodor-Mainvielle.

"No, I couldn't!" protests Fodor-Mainvielle. "Not just before going onstage, Isabella!"

"Oh, be a devil! Just a sip," says Isabella, who has no intention of being deflected. "Do you a power of good." And she almost pours it down the throat of Fodor-Mainvielle.

The orchestra is playing from Rossini's Semiramide. Fodor-Mainvielle moves on stage to an enthusiastic welcome from the partisan Parisian audience. She opens her mouth and sings. Her voice lasts for ten bars of music when it suddenly cracks and then, just simply, stops. She stares at the conductor in disbelief, opens her mouth again to continue, but nothing comes out. Not a note. Not a sound. The orchestra winds down and falls silent. The audience is hushed. No one moves in the theatre. Fodor-Mainvielle rushes off stage.

Fodor-Mainvielle stands in the middle of her dressing-room, wringing her hands then slapping her face violently with both hands. Gioacchino rushes in with a glass of water. Fodor-Mainvielle takes a mouthful and gargles loudly, spits it out onto the floor, opens her mouth to try a note, changes her mind, takes another swig of water, gargles loudly again, and spits it out. She pauses, then opens her arms and her mouth to sing. And emits a croak. There is silence – except for the sounds of a weeping Gioacchino.

Gioacchino has no choice, does he? He has to find a dazzling, coloratura soprano immediately, to play the role of Semiramide, a soprano who has the voice, the range, who knows the score, who has the experience, who is available... and there, in his apartment, in his bathroom, in his bed, there happened to be one Isabella Colbran. Even though, he admitted, she has a slight tendency to sing a little off-key sometimes, just sometimes. He was so fortunate.

She'll think about it, she says. No one likes to be second choice, she says. Especially someone of my stature, she says. An artisan maybe, she says, but not someone of her stature, she says. Semiramide is a queen, after all.

"Ah, well then," says Gioacchino, "I suppose I'll have to look…"

"But seeing as I am here," she says, "and your need is so desperate, and the terms would be so, so generous, wouldn't they?… I may just possibly consider…"

And so Semiramide's season resumes.

It is a great success, lauded by reviewers, the opera public, and even contemporary musicians and composers, despite Isabella's singing, which reviewer, Stendhal, in a complete volte-face to his reaction to Isabella's 'Elizabetta', just over seven years earlier, now describes her performance as "laying waste with the noble ruins of her voice", and during which the more discerning of the opera-goers, "chat amongst themselves until it is over, or else escape outside into a coffee-house and eat ices". Including Giacomo Meyerbeyer.

Meyerbeer is a good-natured but pedestrian musical rival of Gioacchino's. He attends an early performance of Semiramide and is so enraptured by the opera, that he returns the next evening, but abruptly leaves during Isabella's aria, "Quel mesto gemito', and does not return again.

Instead, he employs two impeccably dressed, handsomely paid, elderly gentlemen, to arrive early to each performance, sit in a well-appointed box close to the stage, and visibly fall asleep within the first fifteen minutes of the curtain rising. They would snore loudly at irregular intervals, especially during the more tender moments and, apart from a momentary awakening early on in Act One when a thunderclap greets Semiramide's approach to Ninus' tomb, when they jerk awake, with suitable exclamations, and fall asleep again. They remain in slumber throughout the rest of the performance, only to finally wake when roused by an usher at the end of the opera.

Isabella rages at Gioacchino, demanding he refuse entry to "Les sommeliers de Meyerbeer", as they have become known, or at least have them removed.

Maestro disagrees, in private to Gioacchino. He likes "Les sommeliers", he says, and argues that they at least snore in tune.

But Gioacchino has his own response to the sleepers. He sends two tickets to Meyerbeer for a forthcoming performance of the opera, and attaches a note.

Please do me the favour of using these tickets yourself. The box is visible from all parts of the house. The chairs are comfortable. Shortly before the end of the performance, I shall have you waked.

Your true admirer,
G. Rossini

A few days later, Gioacchino and Meyerbeer meet, quite by accident, and Meyerbeer asks after Gioacchino's health.

"Shaky, dear maître, shaky," replies Gioacchino. "My digestion, you know, my poor head. Alas, I'm afraid I am going downhill."

As soon as Meyerbeer is out of earshot, Maestro materialises alongside Gioacchino. "How could you tell such lies?" he asks. "You have never known better health and yet you talk about going downhill."

"Ah well," says Gioacchino. "Why shouldn't I put it like that? It gives him such pleasure, and just a little hope."

FIFTY-FIVE

France

A restaurant. Rue de Rivoli. Paris

Maestro is seated at his usual Paris table enjoying a favourite cassoulet, and drinking a glass of Bordeaux wine.

Isabella enters, walks up to his table, picks up the plate he is eating from, and tips it all over his face and clothes, then rubs it in. Maestro lurches to his feet.

"You leech!" she hisses, "You treacherous, scheming old leech! You only live when you're sucking the blood of others. When you're sucking the blood of Gioacchino, my Gioacchino!"

Maestro wipes his hands down his clothes and makes an even bigger mess. He looks up at her. "Your Gioacchino!" he laughs. "He's never been your Gioacchino! He's been every woman's Gioacchino. Every woman who's been prepared to drop her skirts for him. And there have been mountains of skirts all over the floor, in many countries, my dear Isabella."

"I am not your dear Isabella!"

"No, you are not. You are a has-been, madame. You're an over-the-hill, out-of-tune, one-time diva, madame. And, Gioacchino only married you for your dowry, in the first place."

"Aagh!" cries Isabella and she throws the contents of Maestro's wine glass on top of the food on his face and chest. She storms out.

Maestro sits again at his table, and summons a waiter. "A bottle of your special Bourgogne 22, if you please, waiter – and, some serviettes, if you wouldn't mind."

And he smiles.

FIFTY-SIX

France

Le Café Anglais. Paris

For the première of Gioacchino Rossini's grand opera, 'Guillaume Tell", chefs around Paris prepared an apple tart with an arrow of sugar decorating the top.

However, the opera itself receives a mixed reception. In its defence, its supporters applaud the scale of the action as heroic, the wonderful tunes that people whistle and play long after they have left the theatre, the tenor role of Arthur is prodigious, especially his aria, 'Asile hereditère', the wonder of the bel canto singing of Mathilde and Arthur in Act Two, and the fact that it is written in French!

The detractors mention the fact that it is written in French, and not Italian, the language of opera, created by God – this from Italians, of course, that it is five hours long, requires vast, scenic stage apparatus, a nightmare for any conductor, and impossible demands on the said tenor role of Arnold.

Overall, a qualified success, that Gioacchino celebrate in the famed restaurant, Le Café Anglais.

Domenico Barbaja had been invited to be present but had regretfully declined, along with his Milanese friend who had bet Gioacchino two truffle-stuffed turkeys that "Guillaume Tell" was never going to happen because it was too long and was about some little-known Swiss patriot whom no one in the world of music and culture cared a jot about. Having lost the bet, once it was clear that the opera would in fact be staged, the friend had tried to get out of paying the bet, by saying that no good truffles were to be had that season.

"No, no," Rossini had responded, "that's a lie put out by turkeys who don't want to be stuffed."

So they dine at Le Café Anglais, the next night, Gioacchino holding forth at the head of the table of artists and dignitaries, Maestro at a side table, almost not there.

Gioacchino requires the chef to prepare a special meal at the table, which he does. The dish is sautéed filet mignon on buttered toast, topped with a slice of foie gras and truffles, and finished with a sauce made from veal stock, the pan juices of the filet deglazed with Madeira, chopped truffles, and butter.

A mere soupçon, as Maestro later describes it.

Unfortunately, because the specified dish is Gioacchino's own creation, he keeps interrupting the chef with instructions and special requests as he cooks. The exasperated chef finally asks to be allowed to cook the dish without his every move being watched and commented on.

"Well, if you don't like it, turn your back," cries Gioacchino.

His guests are delighted with this riposte and name the dish, 'Tournedos alla Rossini' from the French, 'tournez le dos' in memory of the occasion.

This is the story that Gioacchino relates afterwards anyway to Isabella, as she is not present at the opera opening, or at the dinner afterwards. She is not singing in the opera itself, of course, so has little interest, plus, she says, she has to leave early for Italy, on urgent business, the following morning.

FIFTY-SEVEN

Northern Italy

A carriage on the open road

A carriage is travelling at speed on the open road. It approaches a house, set apart from others. The carriage stops. Carlo gets out and holds the carriage door open. Isabella steps down. She is hefting a fairly large bag.

"Wait here," she barks and she moves towards the house.

The house is pitch dark. Isabella takes out a bar from the bag, breaks the lock and forces the door open. She strikes a tinder box and flares a taper. She enters, picks up a lamp from a table and lights it from the taper. She looks around the room and then begins a search. She opens drawers, cupboards, and finally comes across a desk. It is locked. She finds a knife and prises it open. She places the lamp so that she can search thoroughly with both hands.

She finds letters, glances at them, mutters "Gioacchino!" to herself, then discards them. She forces open a locked drawer and takes out letters wrapped in a silk ribbon. She unties the ribbon and reads out loud, "My dearest Wolfi ... I am staying in Baden Baden for a few more weeks. Eat well and look after your health, dear husband, for we need you strong …" Isabella scans down to the end of the letter, and mouths, "Signed, 'Stanzi'".

"Stanzi?" She picks out another letter. "My dear Wolfgang. Fraulein Weber is probably as delightful a young woman as you say she is, but, I strongly suggest …" and again, she skips to the end "… Your loving father, Leopold."

Isabella is starting to realise what she is reading and becomes very excited and agitated. She drops the letters and searches again, and comes across a manuscript, and as she opens it and reads it, she is joined by strings. She throws it down and searches furiously and finds another score that, as soon as she opens it, soars with 'Der Hölle Rache' from Mozart's 'Die Zauberflöte'. Isabella staggers back against the table.

"Holy Mother!" she gasps, "Holy Mother of God!"

FIFTY-EIGHT

France

A street. Paris

Isabella is in very good spirits. She is humming as she is walking, to Gioacchino's great annoyance. Then to Gioacchino's great relief, they are intercepted by Charles Duponchel, Director of Paris Opera.

Duponchel embraces Gioacchino warmly. "My dear Gioacchino! How delightful to meet you and your good lady wife. Madame …" He kisses her hand. "I was talking to my fellow directors of the Paris Opera about you only this morning!"

"Were you?"

"Yes. I was saying that our dear friend Gioacchino Rossini would have little to complain about the Opera Directorate – we're giving Act Two of your Guillaume Tell once again this evening."

"Really? All of it? The whole Act?"

Duponchel is a little confused by this reaction, but plows on, "Yes, as I said …"

"With a ballet, in the second half, I suppose," interrupts Gioacchino.

"Yes, we find the audience loves the combination of …"

"But not too much of the Guillaume Tell, right, sir? Not Acts One, Three and Four?" Gioacchino is relentless. "Just Act Two – sorry, the whole of Act Two, you said, yes?"

Duponchel is non-plussed. "Yes, as I was saying …"

"Good day to you, sir!" says Gioacchino and he strides off.

Isabella follows but cannot resist turning and giving Duponchel a little wave. She hurries and catches up with Gioacchino. "Have you heard the nickname Parisians have concocted for you, my dear?"

"Nickname? What nickname?" he barks, not looking at her.

"They call you Crescendo … Monsieur Crescendo."

He stops and stares at her. "Monsieur Crescendo?"

"Yes, now I wonder why they'd call you that, seeing as you're such a calm, quiet, little person?"

Gioacchino snorts and strides off.

Gioacchino sits at the table in their rooms in their Paris apartment and stares at the table, fuming.

Isabella stands next to him. She sighs lightly, then sighs again, a little louder as Gioacchino seems not to have heard her first sigh. He looks up at her, clearly irritated. Isabella sits down opposite him at the table. She bends her head down low so she can look up into his face. "Did you hear what Donizetti said the other day?" she says, all brightness and cheerfulness.

"No, what did Donizetti say?" Gioacchino asks, and he looks down at the table again, wanting her to know that he does not wish to play her little games.

"That," continues Isabella, "although the first, third and last acts of Guillaume Tell were obviously written by Rossini, it was God who wrote the second Act." She smiles up at him again. "God. But I know it wasn't God. I know who wrote Act Two."

Gioacchino's head snaps up. "Do you? And who was that?"

"Mozart," she says, and smiles.

"Mozart?"

"Yes, Wolfgang Amadeus Mozart. Maestro. Your friend. They're one and the same person."

"Are you mad, woman?" Gioacchino laughs out loud and shakes his head at the stupidity of the woman. "Mozart died over thirty years ago!"

"Did he indeed? Then you explain this!" she exclaims, and tosses a letter down in front of him. "Look there!" She stands and stabs a finger down on the bottom corner of the letter ... where it is signed, 'Wolfgang Amadeus Mozart'. It's a letter to his wife, Costanze. Remember her? And there are lots more ..." and she picks up a bag at her feet, tips it upside down, and spills a cascade of letters onto the table.

"Where did you get these?"

Isabella sits down again and leans back in her chair. "Where did I get them?" She leans forward. "I stole them – from your beloved Maestro. From his house."

"You stole them from his house? You stole them?"

Isabella does not answer. She waits for the news to sink in.

"Anyway," continues Gioacchino, "this does not mean that Maestro is Wolfgang …"

"Oh, but it does!" she cries. "Because here's one of his letters to you … and another … which I stole from you!" She selects a letter from the pile on the table and tosses it down in front of Gioacchino. "The writing is the same! Identical. Look at them!"

He stares down at the letters without touching them.

Isabella picks up one and forces him to acknowledge it. She rubs it into his face. "Think!" she cries, "It fits! It makes complete sense!"

"These could be forgeries! It's easy to copy …"

Isabella jumps to her feet, opens the door to the cupboard behind her and pulls out a fistful of manuscripts. "Forgeries? How else could he have Mozart's music …" and she throws the manuscripts onto the table, "… originals, mind you? How else could he have known so much, been so helpful, so… what were the words you spouted at me earlier… 'outrageous concepts', wasn't that it? Yes, it was! How else could he have written your music with you, for you, my dear Gioacchino? Have you ever thought about that? Have you?"

Gioacchino has gone white. He picks up a manuscript and stares at it in disbelief, in horror. Then another. And another. And another.

"Admit it!" she screams, flecking spit onto his face. "Admit it!"

"Enough!" he breathes. "Enough!" he screams, and he leaps to his feet, sweeps the letters and manuscripts onto the floor, turns and flees the room.

Isabella watches him go, and smiles. "As you say, Gioacchino," she says softly. 'Enough!'"

FIFTY-NINE

France

A bordello. Paris

In a corner of a Parisian bordello sprawls the figure of Gioacchino Rossini. He is leaning forward over a table. He is dirty, haggard, and dishevelled. He has days' growth of beard, and he is clearly drunk. He is counting out a pile of coins on the table in front of him. He is piling them high.

A young prostitute, approaches him and leans over the table towards him, her hanging breasts disturbing the pile of coins. They fall over. Gioacchino screams and lurches to his feet. He grabs a fistful of the coins, throws them at the girl and staggers past her as she scrambles to pick up the coins before anyone else does, and lurches out the door.

SIXTY

France

Gioacchino and Isabella's apartment. Paris

Isabella is seated at her dressing table, applying rouge to her cheeks. Carlo stands behind her.

"You know where Maestro lodges?" she says.

"Yes."

"Then finish it. Tonight." She turns and looks directly at him. "In fact... now."

Carlo turns and exits.

SIXTY-ONE

France

Maestro's apartment. Paris

Maestro walks unsteadily across the room to his bedroom washstand. He is wearing trousers, a shirt that is open, undone, and his feet are bare. He is unshaven. He leans against the stand and wipes the sweat from his face and neck with his hands. He coughs, carefully, with difficulty. He dips his hands into the basin and scoops water over his head, face and neck.

Gioacchino enters behind him, stops and watches.

Unaware that anyone is there, Maestro lowers his head fully into the water.

"Why?" says Gioacchino softly.

Maestro does not hear him.

"Why?" says Gioacchino again, louder.

Maestro jerks up his head, spraying water in an arc, as he is suddenly aware of a voice behind him.

"Why?" comes again.

Maestro stares at Gioacchino, making no attempt to wipe his head, face or neck. "Why what?"

"Why did you do it?" asks Gioacchino.

"Why … why did I do what?"

Gioacchino laughs softly. He continues to laugh as he moves slowly towards Maestro, then speaks as he walks, spiccato. "You died. You were buried. They tossed your body into a pit, with paupers, and threw lime over you. Don't you remember?"

Maestro does not answer. He stares at Gioacchino.

"But you didn't stay buried, did you?" Gioacchino asks, voice still soft, scherzando, "You rose up. Like Lazarus. How did you do that?"

"It wasn't my body," says Maestro.

"It wasn't your body," says Gioacchino, and he moves closer. "Wasn't your body? Whose body was it, then?"

"I don't know his name. I bought it."

"Oh, Gesù!" exclaims Gioacchino. "You bought it!" Suddenly he is eager, "How much did you pay for it?"

"I … I can't remember."

"But why go to all that bother? Why pretend you were dead? Why couldn't you live on as dear old Wolfgang, eh? eh?"

"A myriad reasons – too many … too many …"

"Tell me!" Sforzando.

Maestro is struggling to speak – he is clearly ill, but he makes a Herculean effort, "Huge debt … Freemasons wanted me dead … wife wanted me dead – she was sleeping with my pupil, Sussmayr, for God's sake! … and then there was Magdalena and the baby … I had to disappear …"

"But you didn't, did you?" says Gioacchino. "You didn't stay disappeared! You crawled out of your little hole and said, 'Wolfie wants to play! Let's find some fool – some young, gullible fool, who thinks he can write music – a ninny! a noddy!"

Then even more eagerly, molto ansioso, he snaps, "How much did you pay for me then?"

"Don't do this, Gioacchino …"

"Don't do this?" screams Gioacchino, finally out of control. "Don't ask why you stole my life? Don't ask who wrote my operas? Don't question where Mozart ends and Rossini begins?"

Maestro forces himself to speak. "You are a great composer, Gioacchino! You would have been …"

"That's it!" screams Gioacchino. "A would-have-been! That's me! You're right! Gioacchino, the celebrated, the famous, would-have-been! Because we'll never know, will we? You stole me from me. You stole my life!" And he turns and staggers and stumbles out the door.

SIXTY-TWO

France

A public park. Paris

Gioacchino is seated on a bench under a tree. He is leaning back, head turned up to the sky, but his eyes are closed.

"Maestro, Mozart," he mutters to himself, without opening his eyes. "Mozart. Maestro. First one, then the other."

A man passes. Gioacchino opens his eyes and thrusts out his two closed fists to the man. "Pick which hand he is in, sir!" he calls. "Go on, choose!"

The man veers away and walks hurriedly on.

Gioacchino opens both hands at the same time. "Both!" he says, "or neither … they cannot be the same. They must not be the same. Or I am damned. Damn you, Maestro! Damn you for all time to come. You couldn't stop, could you? You couldn't let me be the mediocrity I was to become. Because there's the crime of it, Maestro, there's the evil of it – I'll never know! I'll never know what was you, and what was me."

A woman with a child approaches.

Gioacchino stands and calls out to her, "What do you think,

madame? Which is me and which is him? Eh? Eh?"

She increases he pace and passes by quickly.

Gioacchino sits. "Everything that I, Gioacchino Antonio Rossini, have ever written, all my music, all my operas, have been the inspiration of another man, a dead man – a monster come back to life to taunt me and to torment me."

He shakes himself violently. "This way lies madness. Either I am a husk, an empty shell of a man, or I am mad. There is no other alternative. And if I am mad, then I would be better dead." He stands. "Dead."

He walks down the path. A dead man.

SIXTY-THREE

France

Maestro's apartment. Paris

The room is dark. Maestro is lying in bed, sleeping fitfully. A figure enters, carrying a covered lantern. The figure stands close by the bed and raises the lantern, illuminating Maestro's face. He sets the lantern down on a small table at the side of the bed. Carefully, so that he will not disturb the sleeping form, the figure picks up a pillow from the bed. He leans over and suddenly presses the pillow down and firmly over Maestro's face. Maestro heaves against the pressure and struggles to escape. The figure bears down as hard as he can over the struggling body. The struggles begin to weaken when there is a scream from behind them.

"No!" Gioacchino surges forward and hurls himself against the figure. They crash against the wall above the bed and topple to the floor. Gioacchino is crying and sobbing uncontrollably as he desperately fights with the silent man. They roll and twist together on the floor. The man presses his thumbs into Gioacchino's eyes. Gioacchino wraps his hands around the man's throat and squeezes as hard as he can. The man begins to gag, He releases his fingers from Gioacchino's face and tries to pull the hands from his throat. He is failing.

There is a strangled cry from the bed above them, "Stanzi!"

Gioacchino's head jerks up towards Maestro – but he keeps his grip on the man's throat.

The voice comes again. "Stanzi!"

Gioacchino releases the man and moves quickly to Maestro.

"Maestro?" he whispers.

There is coughing and gasping from behind them, low to the floor. Carlo staggers to his feet. He sways behind Gioacchino's back, clutches at his throat, then bolts into the night.

SIXTY-FOUR

France

Maestro's apartment. Paris

Gioacchino is pacing the room outside Maestro's bedroom. He keeps looking at the door. The door finally opens and a man appears in the doorway. He is coat-less, his sleeves are rolled back and he is wiping his hands on a towel.

Gioacchino starts forward, "How is he? Is he ...?"

The doctor hushes him and beckons to him to enter the bedroom. Gioacchino goes in.

Maestro is lying in the bed. The doctor leans over Maestro and wipes the perspiration from his face with a towel, then he moves close to Gioacchino and, sotto voce, whispers, "He is gravely ill, sir. I fear he does not have long."

"Not long?" gasps Gioacchino. "Oh God! It's all my fault – if only I'd got here earlier!"

"It would have made no difference," says the doctor. "Don't blame yourself, my friend. There is nothing you could have done. He has pneumonia."

"Pneumonia?"

"Both lungs. He has been ill for some time, I would say." He goes to Maestro and wipes Maestro's face again. He turns back to look at Gioacchino. "He was delirious earlier, shouting crazy things, but he is calm now."

"Crazy things? What crazy things?"

"He kept calling out a name, 'Stanzi', I think it was. Do you know a 'Stanzi'?"

"No, no I don't."

"Then he started saying that someone was poisoning him. 'Aqua toffana!' he kept shouting. 'She's giving me aqua toffana!' And then, thank God, he fell into a sleep."

"Leave him with me. I'll call if I need you."

"Are you sure? He could …"

"Leave!" says Gioacchino. He hands the doctor a pouch of clinking coins.

The doctor accepts the money, picks up his bag, and leaves immediately.

Gioacchino moves to the bed. He takes Maestro's hands, turns them over and looks at the mutilations, the scars. Then he leans in close and whispers, "Maestro."

Maestro does not stir.

"Wolfgang," whispers Gioacchino.

Mozart opens his eyes and stares at Gioacchino. Mozart tries to say something.

Gioacchino cannot hear the words. He leans closer. "What? What is it?" he says.

"Forgive me," says Mozart.

Gioacchino shakes his head. "No, I will not. I will never forgive or forget what you have done, Wolfgang. You changed my life forever."

"Forgive me."

"My friend," says Gioacchino, "we have a saying in Bologna, 'La madre delle teste di cazzo e sempre incinta'."

And surprisingly, amazingly, Mozart laughs in his throat, weakly, sparingly, but a laugh nonetheless. "Yes, yes ... I have heard it ... 'The mother ... of fools ... is always pregnant'."

And Gioacchino joins him in his laughing. "And I am glad of it," he says. "Thank you, mother, for making such a fool as me. Better a fool in Heaven, than a prince in Hell. You have given me the gift of music, my friend, the gift of creation. You have given me the gift of God. I am the most blessed of men."

Mozart's breath stutters. Gioacchino moves even closer and, with his lips almost touching his friend's face, he breathes, "If ever a man loved a friend, then I love you, Maestro. I have known God. To go on now would be unbearable. Rossini without Maestro is not Rossini."

And Mozart tries to sing but only succeeds in whispering, "Di tanti palpiti ... Mi rivedrai ... ti rivedrò ..."

Gioacchino stares at him. He chuckles, then sings, "Di tanti palpiti ... Mi rivedrai, ti rivedrò ..."

And Mozart joins him so that they sing a whispered, breathy duet, "Mi rivedrai ... ti rivedrò ..."

Gioacchino repeats the refrain more strongly, "Mi rivedrai, ti rivedrò …" Then he stops, realizing he is singing on his own. That Mozart is dead.

He looks at the peaceful body for a long time, then speaks to him as if he were still there, listening, sharing, "Goodbye, my friend. You know, some years ago you tried to give me some advice. 'Don't marry a beautiful woman', you said. 'Marry a sow,' you said. 'Marry a pig of a woman,' you said. Well, my dear friend, I have news for you – that is precisely what I did."

And he begins to laugh, and in the middle of his laughter he says, "I did! I married a sow! A beautiful Spanish sow, named Isabella!" His laughter continues to grow, until he cries.

SIXTY-FIVE

In conclusion

Gioacchino exiled Isabella to Bologna in 1829, into the care of his money-pinching father, Giuseppe, then shortly afterwards, divorced her.

Gioacchino Rossini composed thirty-nine operas in the twenty years from 1809 to 1829.

Gioacchino lived for another thirty-nine years after 1829, and died in 1868. He did not compose another opera in all that time.

Author's Note

The backstory to the writing of the novel

"A Secret Never to be Told"

They cut through my chest with an electric saw, opened my ribcage wide, like a briefcase, and lifted up my heart. They detached and then re-attached two arteries from the front of my chest, to the beating heart, cut out a 22 cm section of vein from my left inner forearm and attached it to the still-beating heart, literally by-passing the three clogged arteries, which they left there, under-performing. Then they drilled holes into the bones of the separated halves of my sternum, pulled the two sides of my chest together, inserted wire loops in the holes, twisted the loops tight, sewed up the skin, and I was done.

The day after the operation, I woke up in an Intensive Care ward with three other heart by-pass recipients. All men.

A young female nurse was staring down at me. She smiled and squeezed my hand. "How do you feel?" she said.

What do you say to a question like that? I thought. I said nothing.

Wasn't sure if I could say anything. I felt removed from my throat.

"Do you want anything?" she said.

I wanted to pee but couldn't tell her.

Another nurse came in. A senior nurse. With epaulettes.

She immediately took charge. She told me they were going to remove the four drainage tubes that were sticking out of my belly and disappearing over the side of the bed. I tried to look down but failed. I decided to take her word for it.

Senior then instructed Junior to pull out one of the tubes from my stomach on the count of three and put the end in a basin to catch any spillage.

"One, two, three!"

Junior whipped out the tube so fast that a gout of blood and ooze sprayed down the wall, in an arc, behind her.

The pain was like nothing I had ever experienced before. Searing hot. Blinding white. And a total surprise.

I gasped and gagged. But, strangely, did not emit any other sound. I should have howled, kicked, vomited. But I didn't do any of those things.

And Senior said, "Good! Perhaps a little slower with the next one, please."

I suddenly found my voice. "Next one?" I gasped.

"Yes," she said, "you were so good with the first – even if it was a little fast – most people react a little, but you didn't at all, so maybe we should do the same with the ..."

"No!" I gasped, "slower is better, definitely better."

"Right you are! Slower it is then. Ready? One, two, three!"

By now, of course, it was an issue of honour. Manliness. Courage. Stupidity. I held my breath as she counted, and the wave of pain and nausea escalated rapidly, reached a peak, then slowly subsided. I wasn't sure if I preferred the slow or the fast version.

"Well done!" This was to Junior, not to me. "Now, just two more …"

And they moved on to the next victim. Lying in the bed next to me. Unsuspecting.

His first scream would have been heard in Hell.

I laughed out loud – I didn't mean to – it slipped out – and I regretted it immediately because the laughing hurt. A lot. I didn't remember much more about that day.

When I next woke, I was out of Intensive Care and in my own room. It was dark - not night - the dark of evening. I could make out blue and white curtains with a little motif, and bland, off-white, hospital furniture.

I was the only occupant of the room. Or so I thought. Because when I looked towards a desk that was slightly behind me to my right, there was an old man sitting at it. In his sixties or early seventies, rotund, hair receding but still long over his ears. He was bent over the desk as if reading or writing. I could only see him out of the corner of my eye, so I moved my bottom very carefully, and turned so I could see the man full on.

He wasn't there. There was nobody there. I faced front again and squinted back. And there he sat at the chair.

"Hello," I said, broken voice, like glass.

The man didn't answer. He didn't move. But he stayed with me, hunched over, all that night, and for the next days, but only when I was on his own, and only when I squinted.

After a week, they told me I was allowed to go home.

A Community Nurse sat down next to me, clipboard on her lap, and checked me off against her list.

"Age?"

"Forty-five."

"Appetite?"

"Small."

"Bowel movements?"

"Small."

She laughed. "Hallucinations?"

I stared at her. "How in God's name did you know that?"

"Hallucinations?"

"Yes. I've been seeing a man – over there in the corner - sitting bent over – writing something - never experienced anything like it before."

"Quite common after this kind of operation."

"Why – because of the drugs?"

"No, doesn't seem to be. People on heart-lung machines are on the same drugs but they usually don't hallucinate. You were considered strong and fit enough – apart from your veins - so your heart wasn't stopped. Hallucinations seem to occur only when the patient's heart is kept beating, and is handled. The surgeon reaches in and lifts your heart out of its sac …"

"Sac? I didn't know hearts came in sacs!"

"Protective sac – kind of membrane – anyway, they attached the arteries to your heart while it was beating – touching it of course - and that seems to have effects afterwards."

"Like hallucinations?"

"Yes – and other things."

"What other things?"

"Look, I don't want to put ideas in your head – everyone's different."

"Are these … effects … permanent?"

"It varies … we don't really know. Have you noticed anything else different?"

"No, not really."

But I was lying. I cried a lot. Not bad cries. Good cries.

Much of what I would have previously regarded as mundane, everyday, was suddenly momentous and moving and beautiful. Astonishingly beautiful. Not because I was glad to be alive – even though I was - but out of sheer wonder at the line, the shape, the colours, the sound, the texture, at the breath-taking newness of it all. Simple things: birds flying and alighting on a branch of the tree just outside the window - especially the moment they stretched out their feet and touched or gripped the branch; the songs they sang, each note separate, new each time they sang; individual drops of rain - that drop and that drop; a child laughing somewhere; and as soon as I got home, music, particularly 'Dove sono' from Mozart's 'Le nozze di Figaro' and 'Nacqui all'affano' from Rossini's 'La Cenerentola' – both sung by women, both pieces demanding extraordinary voices that ranged from deep contralto to coloratura soprano, with agile leaps and runs, over and over. So much amazed me, and with each amazement, came the crying.

They were sobbing cryings. None of your tears-in-the-eyes cryings. We're talking pull-over-to-the-side-of-the-road-and-bawl cries here.

And I had to write. Compelled to. Banks of thoughts. They sang in my head and I had to write them down. And stories. Anecdotes and scenes and characters and plotlines poured out of me. Within days of getting home, I had my wife place a pile of blank sheets of paper and pencils at the side of my bed, in the kitchen, next to the toilet pan - in every room in the house. When the urge came, and it came often, I wrote. I wrote on paper, on walls, arms, hands, legs, napkins, tables, bench tops - anywhere, everywhere. I taught myself to write in the dark for if I turned a light on, my wife would sigh, one of those deep, meaningful sighs, but if I didn't write the thought down, I would lie there awake all night anyway trying to remember it.

My first efforts were a scribble – lines of words on top of earlier lines of words, intertwined, indecipherable. Like a code. Until I learned and trained myself to move my hand, in the dark, a double space down for the next line.

I had no choice. I was driven.

The condition, I discovered later, quite by chance, from a 'New Scientist' magazine, is shared by some people who suffer from severe physical trauma. The condition is called Hypergraphia.

Two years before I had my heart by-pass operation, I was rehearsing the music for my role as Ferrando in Opera New Zealand's production of Verdi's 'Il Trovatore', with the conductor of the opera, Eliano Mattiozzi.

Eliano was an Italian who was living in New Zealand and we were rehearsing in his house in Auckland. At the end of the rehearsal, when the accompanist left, Eliano invited me into the kitchen for a coffee. We had become friends over the months of rehearsing. He made two coffees, picked up his mug, sipped, and casually asked me a question.

"You're a writer, as well as a singer, aren't you?"

"Yes, "I said.

"What would you say if I told you Mozart didn't die on December 5, 1791? That he faked his death and lived on?" he said.

"I can think of a number of reasons why Mozart may have faked his death," I said, "… his debts … the Freemasons he'd alienated … his affairs … his wife's liaisons … but if he'd lived on, you couldn't have kept him quiet. He would have composed music."

"He did and he didn't," he said. "He composed with and through someone else."

"Who?"

"Rossini."

"Gioacchino Rossini?"

"Yes. Gioacchino Rossini, the man who wrote thirty-nine operas in nineteen years."

"Thirty-nine operas …"

"... in nineteen years. Think about that. One man!" he said., and he leaned in close, "or was it two?"

"But you're suggesting much more than that. You're saying that that other, was Wolfgang Amadeus Mozart. A dead man ..."

"... a year before Rossini was born."

"So why? Why Mozart?"

"Because of Mozart's desperate need to disappear. To die in order to live."

"And ...?"

"Their music ..."

"Their music?"

"... especially their operas."

"You've studied their ..."

Eliano placed a hand on each of my shoulders and gently eased me onto a chair, then sat opposite me, close. "From 1982 to 1995," he said, "I was Professor of Music at Conservatorio Statale di Musica di Salerno, and at Conservatorio di Musica Giovanbattista Martini di Bologna ..."

"I wasn't questioning your qualifications, Eliano," I spluttered, "... I was simply asking about the two ..."

"... I know," he said. "But I need to tell you this. Because, in that time in Italy, I conducted productions of Mozart's 'Marriage of Figaro' and Rossini's 'Barber of Seville', and, in the process of learning the scores, living inside the scores, over weeks, months, I started to see the similarities - in their harmonies ... their colours ... their tempi ... their sonorities ... even their pauses ... and then I looked closely at other operas - Rossini's 'The Thieving Magpie', Mozart's 'The Magic Flute', Rossini's 'Cinderella'... and I just knew."

"You just knew ..."

"Yes," he said, and he sat back in his chair. "So, I wondered if you might be interested in writing their story."

"... you wondered if I might be interested ..."

For the next two years, I researched the evidence for Eliano's claim, his assertion. One year focussing on Mozart, one year focussing on Rossini. But then, suddenly, tragically, during that time, Eliano died of a heart attack. Without warning.

I finished my research just before my heart operation, and was looking around for someone I would be happy with, to write the screenplay, using my research material.

Without success.

And five weeks and five days after my operation, I wrote the opening lines of the "Maestro" screenplay. And the words poured out of me. I couldn't stop them coming. It was like they were already there, sitting in my brain, and all I had to do was let them out. Six weeks later, I finished the first draft. It was a Friday. The next morning, I started on my next story cum screenplay. And that pattern, that condition, that obsession, that disease, has repeated itself, over and over, ever since. For over twenty years.

But in those twenty years, a conviction grew in me that I needed to go to Vienna, to see, to hear, to smell, to touch, some of the Vienna that Mozart had known. I wanted to stand in the vestibule of St Stephen's Cathedral, I wanted to walk the paths of St Marx' cemetery and find the pauper burial pit into which Wolfgang was supposedly tipped, I wanted to see inside the Grünangergasse apartments ... and the urge became a compulsive need.

So I did. My wife, Jane, and I, arrived at a pension, in a grey, nineteenth-century stone building, in the district of Steffl, where Mozart had lived, and a few tram stops from central Vienna. The apartment was owned by Francesca, a single woman, whose mother, it turned out, was Austrian, and her father, whom she had never met because he died soon after her birth, was Italian. Francesca was about fifty, attractive, and soon to be a Countess. Because her boyfriend, manfriend, was Count Felix von Richter, she said.

The apartment was spacious, furnished with style and eccentricity – for instance, the huge bathroom, apart from the expected bath, toilet, shower, handbasins, etc, also boasted a free-standing porcelain, single person, male urinal, with a lid.

We got on famously with Francesca. Which was very fortunate, because once she found out why we were in Vienna - Mozart and vestibules and graves and burial pits – she invited her manfriend, Count Felix, to join us for dinner one night, because, she said, his great grandfather once owned the skull of Wolfgang Amadeus Mozart.

You wouldn't have believed it.

And over that dinner, Count Felix told us that a gravedigger had exhumed a corpse ten years after Mozart's burial, kept the skull, and sold it to the Count's great grandfather, who, in turn, many years later, gave it to the celebrated bone-collector, Dr. Hirtle.

Was the skull's DNA ever tested? Yes, many years later again, of course, said Count Felix, by The Armed Forces DNA Identification

Laboratory in Maryland, USA, and the University of Innsbruck, against the DNA of Mozart's sister, Nannerl, and his mother. And not only did the DNA of the skull not match the DNA of Nannerl and her mother, but Nannerl's DNA and her mother's DNA did not match either! So why did he still claim it was Mozart's skull? Because double negatives, he said, do not prove or disprove anything.

A tortuous path indeed.

Jane and I stood in the vestibule at St. Stephen's Cathedral, on those same flagstones as Mozart's supposed coffin, and heard a choir singing in the main body of the Cathedral; we told a convincing story and gained entry to the Grünangergasse apartments; and we walked the paths of the cemetery of St. Marx, and stood over the burial pit, marked by a plaque giving Mozart's name and dates. I got down on one knee and bent close to the ground. I don't know why I did that, but I did, and I heard music, cellos, deep, mellow, faint at first, then louder. I swear I did. I told Jane what I was hearing and suggested she bend close and listen. She did, and said she heard nothing, apart from the distant traffic.

"A Secret Never to be Told" is the novel that came out of the "Maestro" screenplay: the story of Wolfgang Amadeus Mozart and Gioacchino Antonio Rossini, two of the greatest composers the world has ever known.

Lynn John, June 2022

www.ingramcontent.com/pod-product-compliance
Lightning Source LLC
Chambersburg PA
CBHW070651120526
44590CB00013BA/915